MODELS OF ATONEMENT

Speaking about Salvation in a Scientific World

George L. Murphy

George L. Murphy

Lutheran University Press
Minneapolis, Minnesota

MODELS OF ATONEMENT

Speaking about Salvation in a Scientific World
by George L. Murphy

Library of Congress Cataloging-in-Publication Data

Murphy, George L., 1942-
  Models of atonement : speaking about salvation in a scientific world /
George L. Murphy.
      pages cm
  Includes bibliographical references.
  ISBN 978-1-932688-85-6 (alk. paper) — ISBN 1-932688-85-4 (alk. paper)
  1. Creation. 2. Religion and science. 3. Jesus Christ—Crucifixion. 4.
Salvation—Christianity. I. Title.
  BS652.M87 2013
  234—dc23

                                        2013003333

Lutheran University Press, PO Box 390759, Minneapolis, MN 55439
www.lutheranupress.org
Manufactured in the United States of America

CONTENTS

PREFACE

The first article that I published in what has come to be called the science-theology dialogue appeared in 1977. At that time not a lot was being done in this area, and most pastors and teaching theologians considered it at best a topic to be left to some specialists. That has changed considerably in the past third of a century, and now there are many journals, books, conferences, college and seminary courses, and organizations devoted to different aspects of the dialogue. Theologians are coming to see its importance, not just as a hobby or sideline but as an integral part of the theological enterprise. If God is indeed the creator of the world then the kind of knowledge that science can give us about the world will be helpful and in fact necessary for our attempts to understand both God's original creative work and God's ongoing activity in the universe.

Sometimes when I have given talks about science and theology to groups of clergy and laity, one of the things asked in the question period has been, "What does this have to do with the gospel?" It is not an unreasonable thing to wonder. Most of the discussions about relationships between science and Christianity have focused on the doctrine of creation. Attempts to understand biological evolution in the context of Christian belief about God as the creator of all things is in fact the first thing that comes to many people's minds when they hear the phrase "religion and science," with big bang cosmology perhaps a close second. How to understand God's action in the world, implications of the sciences for anthropology and concerns about the environment are other matters that come under the broad heading of creation. And these topics are all quite interesting. But what does the discussion have to do with the central Christian message—the gospel proclamation that we are saved, reconciled to God, through the life, death, and resurrection of Jesus of Nazareth?

In comparison with discussions of creation and science, not a great deal has been written about salvation and science. It has to be confessed that Christians who oppose evolution, in their attempts to show that acceptance of it is heretical, have done more to relate these topics than have those who for whom evolution is not a problem. These attempts are tragically wrong, insistent as they are on reading scripture in naïve ways and denying overwhelming scientific evidence about the world, but at least their proponents try to make some connection between the heart of the Christian claim and science. Mainline theologians have often failed to do so and, to the extent that is the case, science-theology dialogue will be on the periphery of the church's concern. And that, in turn, will make the church's message seem increasingly out of synch with the way that scientifically literate people think.

In an earlier book, *The Cosmos in the Light of the Cross* (Trinity Press International, 2003), I set out an approach to theological understanding of science and technology based on aspects of Luther's theology of the cross. Luther's concern in developing that theology had to do primarily with issues that engaged the church at the time of the Reformation—sin, law, righteousness, and salvation. In the sixteenth century the doctrine of creation was not in dispute in significant ways. The theology of the cross does, however, also have important implications for our knowledge of God and our understanding of God's action in the world, and those were the issues that I concentrated on in my earlier work. In this book I return to Luther's primary concern: discussing the atoning work of Christ (in continuity with my previous work) that related belief in creation with scientific knowledge of the world.

My purpose here is not to present a "scientific theory of the atonement," whatever such a thing might be. It is instead to present a way of understanding the atonement that makes contact with a scientific understanding of the world. I am not arguing that this is the only legitimate way to think about the work of Christ, but it has, I believe, the merit of making Christian claims about salvation comprehensible in a culture that is heavily influenced by science and for people who are accustomed to thinking of their world and their lives in scientific language. Thus I hope that this book can be a resource for preachers and educators in the church, enabling them to express the gospel in ways that are appropriate for a scientific age.

While my primary theme is the saving work of Christ, it will be necessary to look at the problem that requires that work, human sinfulness. Traditional ideas about original sin, key components of Christian theology, have been challenged on the basis of evolution, and many people have argued that if there was no "fall" of an historical Adam and Eve, then the whole concept of the atoning work of Christ becomes pointless. We will see that such arguments are greatly overstated, but it will be important to develop an understanding of sin that recognizes evolution as the means through which God has created us but does not make God the creator of sin. See Chapter IV for this discussion.

I have developed some of these concepts in earlier articles, references to which are given at appropriate points. I am grateful to the Biologos Foundation for making available (at http://biologos.org/uploads/projects/murphy_scholarly_essay.pdf) my essay "Human Evolution in Theological Context," which summarizes basic ideas in the present book. Thanks are also due to David Congdon, Peter Dahl, Terry Gray, Dan Harlow, Judi Huseth, Denis Lamoureux, Steve Martin, David Opderbeck and Sandra Selby for conversations, criticism and encouragement, both in person and online, in the course of my work. I am also indebted to Duane Priebe, in whose soteriology class at Wartburg Seminary many years ago some of the ideas that I have developed here germinated. And as in my earlier work, the support, criticism, encouragement and proofreading of my wife, Dona Chadwick Murphy, have been invaluable.

The discussion of "atonement as actual event" by the late Gerhard Forde in Locus 7, "The Work of Christ," of *Christian Dogmatics* (Fortress, 1984) edited by Carl Braaten and Robert Jenson plays a central role in my own treatment of the work of Christ, especially in Chapter VI. I am happy to acknowledge my indebtedness to Forde's work, though I take full responsibility for the way I have made us of it.

Unless otherwise noted, biblical citations are from the New Revised Standard Version (NRSV). Where possible, patristic references are to *The Ante-Nicene Fathers* or *The Nicene and Post-Nicene Fathers* (Wm. B. Eerdmans, Grand Rapids, 1979 reprint), cited as ANF and NPNF, followed (in the latter case) by the series number.

CHAPTER I

SALVATION AND SCIENCE

Views of the Atonement

"Christ died for our sins in accordance with the scriptures."

Just a few years after Jesus of Nazareth had died on a Roman cross outside the walls of Jerusalem, Saul of Tarsus, who had recently been brought to accept the claim that Jesus had been raised from the dead and was the Messiah, received the early Christian tradition about the death and resurrection of Christ from the community of Jesus' disciples in Jerusalem. Sometime after that, in the mid-50s of the first century, he passed on that tradition to the church at Corinth in the fifteenth chapter of his first letter to that congregation. The tradition which he quoted begins with the opening sentence of this paragraph and continues with testimony to Jesus' burial and appearances of the risen Christ to witnesses (1 Corinthians 15:3-7).

This primitive Christian tradition has been subjected to a great deal of study, usually in connection with Jesus' resurrection. We will consider that in due time, but we begin with Jesus' death on a cross. The fact that he died is not in itself remarkable, but it is notable that, from the standpoint of their belief that he had indeed been raised, his first disciples could say that that death was "for our sins." In view of later controversies it is important to emphasize that that is not in the remotest sense a late theological development. The belief that Jesus' death was somehow effective in solving the problem of human sin was part of the earliest Christian proclamation.

The New Testament writers, of course, not only repeated this claim but expanded upon it. In another letter Paul wrote that Jesus "was handed over to death for our trespasses and was raised for our justification" (Romans 4:25), while 1 Peter 2:24a says, "He himself bore our sins in his body on the cross, so that, free from sins, we might live for righteousness" and 1 John 1:7 tells us that "the blood of Jesus [God's] Son cleanses us from all sin." This line of thinking attains its greatest scope in the Christ hymn of Colossians (1:15-20), which concludes with the statement that "through him God was pleased to reconcile to himself all things whether on earth or in heaven, by making peace through the blood of his cross." But the fundamental belief that the death of Christ was in some way "for our sins" came very early to Jesus' followers, well before there had been any detailed theological reflection on the idea.

The history of translation of a verse from another of Paul's letters provides us with a word that has been used frequently in discussions of the significance of Christ's death. The NRSV translation of 2 Corinthians 5:19 reads, "That is, in Christ God was reconciling the world to himself, not counting their trespasses against them, and entrusting the message of reconciliation to us." In Tyndale's version of 1525 (a critical step in the trajectory that leads through the King James Version to the NRSV), the last clause reads "and hath comitted to us the preaching of the attonement."[1] Tyndale apparently coined the word "attonement" (whose spelling has since been altered slightly) to mean "reconciliation."[2] In this case popular etymology is correct: The word is simply "at-one-ment." It is important to keep this in mind because the word "atonement" has come to be connected with particular understandings of the way in which reconciliation is brought about. "Day of Atonement" as a translation of *yom kippur* or the phrase "blood atonement" of popular theology are examples. But its fundamental meaning is "reconciliation," without any implication of one or another "theory of the atonement" (i.e., theory about the life, death, and resurrection of Christ bringing about reconciliation between God and the world). Atonement has been accomplished when the proper relationship between God and humans has been brought about.

Theories of the atonement will, however, concern us here. In recent years there has been lively discussion and debate among theologians about such attempts to understand the logic of the atonement. The heart of the Christian message has always been that we are saved because of what God has done for us in Jesus Christ and, in particular, through his cross and resurrection. But why are those particular events salvific? What does it mean to be "saved"? What are we supposed to be saved *from*? And what are we saved *for*? The message that "God so loved the world that he gave his only Son, so that everyone who believes in him may not perish but may have eternal life" (John 3:16) can be preached without examining those questions. We do need to address them, however, if we want to explain and support that proclamation so that it makes sense to those who hear it in today's world.

The questions in the previous paragraph should not be dealt with simply as "how" enquiries—that is, as requests for information about the mechanism by which the work of Christ accomplishes its purpose. If they are understood only in that way, the answers we develop are likely to be rationalistic schemes which describe what God and/ or humanity supposedly had to do to accomplish reconciliation. That, in turn, may divert our attention from what Jesus actually did and focus it on the fulfillment of some putative cultic or legal requirements. The late Gerhard Forde presented that criticism with particular cogency. (His argument for "atonement as actual event" will be used in Chapter VI.)[3] While "how" questions should not be neglected entirely, the primary function of a theory of the atonement should be explication of the *meaning* of what God has done and continues to do through the life, death, and resurrection of Christ. It would be better to speak of "models" rather than "theories" of the atonement, but the latter usage is perhaps too well established to be ousted.

Discussions about how Christ saves us go back to the early days of Christianity.[4] The New Testament gives us a number of images of the salvific effectiveness of Jesus' life, death, and resurrection. In a world in which sacrifice was practiced by both Jews and Gentiles it was inevitable that the death of Christ would be spoken of in this way, and the letter to the Hebrews develops in some detail the idea of Christ as the priest "according to the order of Melchizedek" (Hebrews 6:20) who offered himself to God. There are numerous texts that speak of Christ as in some way our substitute. We have already noted Romans 4:25 and 1 Peter 2:24 and could add, among others, Paul's statement in Galatians 3:13 that "Christ redeemed us from the curse of the law by becoming a curse for us." A related idea is that of Christ as our "ransom" (Mark 10:45, 1 Corinthians 6:20). Christ is also pictured as the victor over powers that threaten creation in texts such as Colossians 2:13-15, and as the one who, in the unified cross-resurrection event, will draw all people to himself (John 12:32).

These ideas have their backgrounds in the Old Testament. The sacrificial imagery of Hebrews makes explicit use of the ideas associated with *yom kippur* in Leviticus 16. On the other hand, references to Christ "bearing" our sins (as in the 1 Peter text above or John 1:29) seem to have as their background the scapegoat concept (Leviticus 16:20-22) rather than sacrifice in a narrow sense.[5] The fourth servant song of Isaiah (52:13—53:12), which Philip used as an opportunity to speak about Jesus in Acts 8:26-40, emphasizes that God's servant suffers and dies because God has placed the burden of the people's sins on him, while Paul's claim that Christ became a curse for us is based on the statement in Deuteronomy 21:23 that "anyone hung on a tree is under God's curse." The picture of Christ as victor (including the story of him walking on the sea in Mark 6:47-52 and parallels) calls to mind the image of the *Chaoskampf*, God's battle with primordial sea monsters symbolic of the chaos that threatens creation in Old Testament texts such as Psalm 89:8-13.

The church fathers of course discussed these texts in attempts to understand more fully the work of Christ. The image of ransom, for example, raised questions. To whom was the ransom paid: God or the devil? Both answers seem problematic. Why would a loving God require payment before freeing God's creatures from bondage? On the other hand, does the devil have any "rights" to dominion over humanity that God would be bound to respect?

The first really systematic attempt to develop what would come to be called a theory of the atonement was that of Anselm of Canterbury at the end of the eleventh century in his treatise *Cur Deus Homo*, "Why God Became Human."[6] Here he argued that human sin had given infinite offense to the honor of God by threatening the divine purpose for creation. God became human so that a human life of infinite value could be offered to satisfy the divine honor and make it possible for God's purpose to be achieved. Anselm's understanding of the atonement was soon challenged by Peter Abelard, who argued for what has come to be called a "subjective" or "moral influence" theory:[7] The love of God displayed in Jesus' death on the cross evokes a corresponding love in us. Those views and their variants have been debated ever since the twelfth century. The idea of "penal substitution," which has some resemblance to Anselm's view but is rather different in its emphasis, has continued to be quite influential.

In 1931 Gustaf Aulén's *Christus Victor* re-introduced another partner into these debates.[8] As the book's title indicates, Aulén argued that the ancient motif of Christ as the victor over sin, death, and the devil should be seen as one major view of the work of Christ, and that it was in fact superior to the "Latin" and "subjective" views in several ways. While his arguments have, of course, not been accepted by all theologians, Aulén's book has established patterns for much of the later discussion of the atonement. Modern treatments of the work of Christ often set out a number of different "types" of atonement theories or models that they discern in Christian history, pointing out strengths and weaknesses, and then either express their own preferences or argue that a variety of images and motifs should be retained.[9] Other theologians make clear from the start that they consider a particular understanding of atonement to be correct and then go on to support it and deal with criticisms. Evangelicals in particular have generally argued for the concept of penal substitution—the idea that Christ suffered in the place of sinners the punishment that God's retributive justice required.[10]

Debates about different theories or models of atonement have been going on for a long time, but in recent years a new factor has been introduced. The label "anti-redemptionism" has been given to the "unorthodoxy" of those who consider themselves followers of Jesus but who hold that the whole idea of atonement through his death is misguided.[11] (Thus "anti-redemptionists" in this sense do not include those who simply reject all of Christianity.) The idea that God would make use of the violence of the cross and the supposed implication of "divine child abuse" involved in the idea of God sending his Son to suffer and die have offended especially some feminist theologians. Penal substitution has been a particular target of such criticisms. At the same time, some biblical scholars have pictured Jesus as a prophet and wisdom teacher whose crucifixion was due simply to the challenge he presented to Roman authority and not "the definite plan and foreknowledge of God" (Acts 2:23).[12] A variation on these ideas, which cannot really be called anti-redemptionist, is the "Narrative Christus Victor" model of J. Denny Weaver.[13]

It is now quite common for writers dealing with atonement to emphasize the social context in which different ideas have developed. (In fact, the need for contextualization is now recognized by theologians quite generally.) Anselm's proposal about the need to provide satisfaction for the damage done to God's honor by sin, for example, made more sense in the feudal society of medieval Europe than it does in twenty-first century America. An early presentation of this role of social context throughout history in understanding the death of Christ was Shailer Matthews' 1930 work *The Atonement and the Social Process*.[14] Matthews was far too dismissive of traditional Christian ideas such as divine sovereignty and human guilt. Nevertheless, his argument that Christianity in a scientific world needs an understanding of the death of Christ that is different from the cultic, legal, and political ideas of the past is even more true today than it was eighty years ago.

Related ideas were expressed by Paul Tillich in his analysis of different types of anxiety—that of fate and death, of emptiness and meaninglessness, and of guilt and condemnation.[15] While Tillich made it clear that these three types cannot be completely separated and assigned uniquely to specific historical periods, it is true that the fear of death and corruption was predominant in the time of the early church while the time of the Reformation was marked by concern about guilt and divine judgment. Today the fear that we live meaningless lives in a universe devoid of purpose is for many people the result of reflection on what they see as the results of scientific study. The words with which Steven Weinberg, a Nobel laureate in physics, closed his popular presentation of scientific cosmology are well known: "It is almost irresistible," he wrote, "for humans to believe that we have some special relationship to the universe, that human life is not just a more-or-less farcical outcome of a chain of accidents reaching back to the first three minutes, but that we were somehow built in from the beginning." Weinberg did resist that belief, however. "The more the universe seems comprehensible," he says, "The more it also seems pointless."[16]

Doing Theology in a Scientific World

An indispensable guideline for the work of the Christian church in the twenty-first century is a statement made by John Mangum as he introduced a collection of essays from a conference on science and Christianity in 1989: "[T]oday's churches have no other place to fulfill their mission than a world whose basic assumptions are pervaded more and more by science."[17] If we are to be effective in addressing questions about the fundamental human problem and God's answer to it, we have to take into account the fact that in a scientific culture the understanding of the world and of themselves which informed people have is increasingly phrased in scientific terms and comprehended in the context of scientific knowledge.

The subject of "science and religion" has flourished in recent decades perhaps even more than have discussions of atonement. The old notion that there must be inevitable "warfare" between religion and science is now held (though sometimes rather loudly) only by those on the atheistic or fundamentalist fringes. Today there are numerous books, journals, conferences, college and seminary courses, and organizations devoted to the study and discussion of different aspects of the relationship between science and religion. In particular, there are now extensive conversations among Christian theology, ethics, science and science-based technology—what has come to be called the science-theology dialogue for short.

The focus of this dialogue has been primarily on issues related to the theological concept of creation. Origins—cosmic, biological, and human—as well as God's ongoing activity in the world, *creatio continua*, have been the subject of extensive discussions, with biological evolution receiving special attention. Calls to care for creation have been one result of environmental theologies, and advances in biological knowledge and medical practice have provoked new reflections on human nature and produced new ethical challenges.

Relatively little attention, however, has been given to issues related to salvation and to what is supposed to have been accomplished through the cross and resurrection of Christ.[18] And since salvation through Christ is the heart of the good news that the church is called to proclaim, a neglect of that topic in science-theology dialogue seems to suggest that it has only secondary importance for the mission of the church. Writing about and discussing the relationships between big bang cosmology or biological evolution and theology may be all right for those who like that kind of thing, but many parish pastors think that it isn't really necessary for the task to which they are called, the proclamation of the gospel.

The relative neglect of soteriology in science-theology dialogue has been matched by rather scanty consideration of scientific matters in studies of atonement. Discussions of sin and salvation even by today's critical mainline theologians may still refer to "Adam" and fail to give any attention to what has been discovered about the evolutionary development of humanity from pre-human ancestors. Certainly Adam— and Eve—may be understood as theological representations of the earliest humans. But it should be obvious that any discussion of concepts such as the sinful condition of human beings and salvation from that condition must take into account what science tells us about humanity as evolved creatures if it is to refer to the real world.

Our concern is not just with a general disconnect that many people have felt between traditional Christian ideas about salvation and the scientific picture of the world that has developed over the past four and a half centuries. Specific challenges have been directed at traditional doctrines and, not surprisingly, the contributions of Copernicus and Darwin have been seen as major stumbling blocks for any kind of orthodox theology. In 1832 Ralph Waldo Emerson wrote, "I regard it as the irresistible effect of the Copernican astronomy to have made the theological *scheme of Redemption* absolutely incredible."[19] More recently, tension between traditional Christian ideas of a primordial state of human innocence and a "fall" into depravity on one hand, and scientific knowledge about how evolution works and the knowledge about early humans inferred from studies of primate behavior on the other, is supposed to have made the concept of atonement meaningless. John Spong put it this way.

> As post Darwinians, we no longer believe we were created perfect. We were created as single cells of life and evolved into our present complex, conscious and self-conscious forms. Since we were never perfect, we could not fall into sin. Since we could not fall into sin, we could not be rescued. How can one be rescued from a fall that never happened or be restored to a status we never possessed?[20]

Such arguments are not new. They have long been used by nonbelievers in attacks on traditional Christianity as well as by Christians who reject the idea of human evolution.

But as Bishop Spong's statement shows, they can also be made by those within the Christian camp who accept evolution. The type of "anti-redemptionism" that appeals to scientific arguments is of particular interest for our discussion, and we will deal with some of its specific arguments in due course.[21]

Broadening of science-theology dialogue to include soteriology and, in turn, inclusion of scientific knowledge in discussions of atonement, can benefit both areas of theology. To begin, we simply need to take seriously the Copernican and Darwinian challenges that were mentioned above. Scientific cosmology and biological evolution are realities for people with even modest scientific training. But beyond the type of apologetic work that scientific discoveries provoke, new approaches to atonement, or just fresh nuances of traditional approaches, may become possible. The science-theology dialogue itself will profit by having a more central role within the whole of Christian theology.

Thus I intend to present here an understanding of the saving work of Christ in a way that is understandable within a modern scientific picture of the world. The realities of human evolution which have seemed, to some, to undermine the whole idea of atonement will be incorporated in this approach in a natural way. In the nature of the case, the challenge posed by Emerson and the consequent questions about the salvation of extraterrestrials will have to be dealt with more speculatively. We do not, after all, know at this time whether or not there are any such creatures.

Purposes, Limits, and Language of the Present Work

The goal here is relatively modest: formulating an understanding of the work of Christ that is grounded in scripture, retains some continuity with the theological tradition, takes seriously today's scientific picture of the world, and uses language that makes contact with that picture. I am not interested, however, in trying to make theology a branch of science.[22] Science, what used to be called "natural philosophy," should have a ministerial role rather than a magisterial one, in theology.[23] Thus I do not propose to develop a "scientific theory of the atonement," as if the work of Christ could be described in its fullness by the natural, human, and social sciences. Except when we make some comparisons between our approach and others, we will seek language that has more in common with scientific discourse than with that of law courts, slave markets, temples, battlefields, and other settings that furnished the conceptualities and metaphors of traditional theories of the atonement. This does not mean, however, that all traditional words such as "righteousness" and "faith" will be eschewed. The language of faith, in fact, will be perhaps even more important here than it is for some other models of atonement.

My interest here is not in simply adding one more book to the library of academic theologians. The whole purpose of theology is to support proclamation of the Word of God, law and gospel. The church's preachers and teachers need to be able to expound the message that "Christ died for our sins in accordance with the scriptures" in ways that makes sense to scientifically literate people and to those who, for whatever reason, find the imagery of other models of the atonement unconvincing. I hope that this book will be able to provide a useful resource for those who are called to this task of proclamation and teaching.

Though our scientific context is of considerable importance for theology, the influence of the sciences on our understanding of salvation will be indirect. What I will argue is that science helps us to understand God's activity in creation and that activity is paralleled in important ways by God's salvific work.

The model to be presented here is not intended as a total replacement of all other ways of thinking about atonement. Pictures of Christ as victor over the powers of evil or as the one who suffers the consequences of our sins will continue to be used in a good deal of preaching and teaching. The point is not to get rid of them but to provide a way of understanding the atoning work of Christ that is understandable in a scientific and technological world.

The biblical concept from which our theory will be developed is that of "new creation." While this precise term (*kainē ktisis*) is used in only two biblical texts (2 Corinthians 5:17 and Galatians 6:15), the idea is implied in other language, such as references to rebirth and promises of new heavens and new earth. In view of the dynamic evolutionary character of the world, new creation will be seen not as a sudden replacement of one static entity by another, and certainly not as a return to some ideal primordial state, but as a re-orientation of the trajectory of creation. Human sin means that creation is moving away from the goal which God intended for it, and the work of Christ will be seen as turning creation back toward its proper end. There is some similarity between this idea and the views of Irenaeus in the second century about Christ's recapitulation of human history, though of course that church father had no idea of modern theories of evolution.

To state the matter in that way assumes that there is indeed a goal or purpose for creation. One of the clearest statements about this, and one that will be discussed in more detail later, is Ephesians 1:10. This refers to God's "plan for the fullness of time, to gather up all things in him [Christ], things in heaven and things on earth."

There are two reasons for making re-creation our starting point. To begin with, it is an expression of an ancient theological theme expressed by Athanasius, one so basic that I have called it "Athanasius' Axiom": "The renewal of creation has been the work of the self-same Word that made it at the beginning."[24] The saving work of Christ is not, as the Gnostics imagined, an intervention to save human souls from the botched work of an inferior creator. It is, rather, the creator of the universe getting creation back on track after creatures have derailed it.

Secondly, as we have seen, science-theology dialogue has explored connections between scientific understandings of the world and theological concepts of creation in some detail. It seems likely that treating atonement in terms of a reorientation or renewal of creation will make it possible for us to build on some of that work and thus make contact with scientific knowledge.

The concept of new creation has not been neglected entirely in other theories of the atonement, though it has often been present only implicitly or seen as a result of the work of Christ though not as a description of what that work actually is. We will explore some other expressions of the idea while presenting a theory in which this concept is central.

Attention will not be given exclusively to the salvation of humans, but the act of reorientation of creation takes place within humanity in the person of Jesus Christ, in his death and resurrection. In order to understand this, and thus to have a "theory of the atonement" in the narrow sense, we turn to Forde's proposal.[25] When the cross-resurrection event is proclaimed to sinners it is a work of new creation because it destroys idolatrous faith and creates true faith in the true God. People who have been moving away from their creator, sometimes deliberately fleeing from God, are turned back to the goal that God wills for them, the ultimate union of "all things" with Christ.

This idea of a reorientation of creation has been developed as part of a concept in which science and technology are understood in the context of a theology of the cross.[26] I have called this "chiasmic cosmology," using Plato's image of the World Soul "placed crosswise (*echiasen*) in the universe," which Justin Martyr in the second century saw as prophecy of the cross that the Greek philosopher borrowed from Moses.[27] (It is the image of Christ crucified present and active throughout the universe that is of interest here, not Justin's conjecture about the source of Plato's idea.) Earlier work in this program, with appropriate references, will be described in the next chapter.

Finally, something needs to be said in this introductory chapter about the language that will be used in the following discussions. There are a number of different terms with different connotations that are commonly used to refer to what Christ's life, death, and resurrection accomplish. I have already discussed the word "atonement" and pointed out its equivalence with reconciliation. Salvation, redemption, and justification are other important words used in the New

Testament and the Christian theological tradition. Atonement or reconciliation are the primary terms that will be emphasized here because they are best suited to express the understanding that the work of Christ enables creation to reach its goal of unity with him,

Salvation has to be understood with reference to what we are saved from, the end result of moving away from God, which is death and destruction. Redemption and justification, on the other hand, are terms derived from, respectively, the practice of purchasing the freedom of slaves or prisoners and legal processes. Those terms are biblical and their appropriateness in the contexts of particular understandings of atonement cannot be denied, but they do not have a natural place in the approach pursued here. The importance of what has been called the doctrine of justification does, however, mean that we will have to be careful that the way we speak of atonement in fact expresses in other language what that doctrine has meant.

Choice of language is of more than literary interest, for different concepts demand different words. The word "guilt" will not play a significant role in our discussions, because the idea of an objective guilt associated with sin is a part of a judicial approach to the question of sin and salvation which we will not pursue. (Of course lack of emphasis on this concept does not mean that people do not feel guilty about what they have done or the type of people they are.) In particular, the concept of "original guilt"—the Augustinian claim that all humans not only inherit effects of an historically first sin such as the tendency to sin but that they are actually guilty of the sin of Adam—does not come into consideration. That idea has seemed troublesome to many Christians, for it has been difficult to see how assigning guilt to one person for another person's crime could be just. We will not wrestle with that problem.

CHAPTER II

"THE CROSS TESTS EVERYTHING"[28]

Theology of the Crucified One

Any adequate Christian theology must in some way be a "theology of the cross." A person who approaches one of the canonical gospels expecting to find something like a conventional biography of Jesus of Nazareth may be surprised at what seems to be an inordinate proportion of the text devoted to the final days of the protagonist and his suffering and death. The Gospel of Mark in particular has been called "a passion narrative with a long introduction."[29] The understanding of Christ that we find in Paul and most of the other New Testament writings is centered on his cross and resurrection. Both formal Christian theology and popular piety have always paid a great deal of attention to the crucifixion of Jesus. It is true that, as recent critics have pointed out, this has sometimes been done in morbid or masochistic ways. On the other hand, an explicit denial of the cross or even a downplaying of its significance represents a fundamental departure from traditional Christianity. Islam, which grants Jesus a very honorable position but denies that he died on the cross, is a prominent example.[30]

For Luther the cross was not just an important part of theology but the foundation of all real theology. His *theologia crucis* is set out most clearly in his theological theses for the Heidelberg Disputation of 1518.[31] As Gerhard Forde emphasized in his exposition of these theses, Luther actually speaks here about what makes a person a "theologian of the cross" rather than what constitutes a "theology of the cross" in the abstract.[32] The cross is a matter of personal and existential importance. While the content of a theology of the cross is essential, it is the procedure which one follows in trying to understand "the teaching about God and divine things"[33] that determines, according to Luther, whether or not one is a Christian theologian.

The one who "deserves to be called a theologian," he says, "comprehends the visible and manifest things of God seen through suffering and the cross."[34]

In view of such statements, it is understandable that Luther described his theses as "theological paradoxes." They systematically challenge common sense understandings of law, righteousness, sin, human abilities, and the character of God. That challenge begins with the first thesis: "The law of God, the most salutary doctrine of life, cannot advance humans on their way to righteousness, but rather hinders them."[35] This is of course contrary to the view of common sense religion, of what Luther calls theologians of glory, that adherence to the law enables us to become righteous.

We come to the heart of the matter in Thesis 20: "That person deserves to be called a theologian, however, who comprehends the visible and manifest things of God through suffering and the cross." We almost automatically look for God in situations of beauty, power, and order. (That is where we would be if we could be God!) The idea that God is to be found in the humiliation, suffering, and death of Jesus on the cross is, as Paul said, "a stumbling block to Jews and foolishness to Gentiles" (1 Corinthians 1:23). It clashes with our "natural" understanding of who God is.

There is no serious debate about the fact that the historical Jesus of Nazareth suffered what Origen called "the utterly vile death of the cross."[36] Simply to honor a human teacher who experienced such a fate would, to a certain extent, be paradoxical. But Christ is, in traditional Christian understanding, both fully human and fully divine. Can we speak of the central crucifixion on Golgotha, with its suffering, god-forsakenness, and death, as an event in which God is really involved—and involved as the victim? Much of traditional Christian theology, influenced by the Greek philosophical tradition and the common sense tendency already mentioned, has held that God is absolutely immutable and impassible and thus incapable of suffering or death. There were exceptions in the early church, the most interesting being the third century bishop Gregory Thaumaturgus. He argued that while suffering cannot be imposed on God from any other agent, God is free to choose to suffer.[37] But such views were not generally held.

Classical theology solved the problem with its understanding of communication of attributes in the hypostatic union. The divine and human natures of Christ are united in the single divine Second Person of the Trinity, and whatever can be said of either nature can be attributed to the person. So while "God in his own nature cannot die,"[38] by assuming human nature the Son of God could truly take on our death.

Thus the problem can to some extent be managed within the context of a belief in divine immutability, but the very fact that we have to treat it as a "problem" is a clue that there is something wrong with that approach. God's full presence in the cross-resurrection event is supposed to be the *solution* to fundamental human problems. The assumptions of divine immutability and impassibility which come from philosophical theism make that solution into a problem to be solved! It is true that we must not simply model God on ourselves and vest the divine with our limitations. But it is at least equally idolatrous to construct a deity with what we imagine to be ideal divine properties. That is the practice of theologians of glory who, Luther says in Thesis 19, do not deserve to be called theologians.

While Luther accepted the decrees of Ephesus and Chalcedon on the incarnation, he pushed the concept of the communication of attributes to, and in some cases beyond, its traditional limits.[39] Marc Lienhard has spoken of the "Dei-passianism" of some of his statements.[40] In the twentieth century the concepts of divine immutability and impassibility were challenged more explicitly by theologians such as Kazoh Kitamori, Jürgen Moltmann, and Eberhard Jüngel.[41] Jüngel in particular has insisted that in order to speak adequately of God today we must be able to speak of deity together with perishability. God does not only act in or reveal Godself through the cross, but is to be *identified* first of all by the cross:

The humanity of this person [Jesus] is extremely relevant to the meaning of the word "God," according to the New Testament view. This is true not just of the life but especially of the death of this person.

> Therefore, when we attempt to think of God as the one who communicates and expresses what God is in the person Jesus, then we must always remember that this man was *crucified*, that he was killed in the name of God's law. For responsible Christian usage of the word "God," the Crucified One is virtually the real definition of what is meant with the word "God." Christian theology is therefore fundamentally the theology of the Crucified One.[42]

The image of God Incarnate entering into death in order to defeat it—"trampling down death by death" in the words of the Orthodox paschal troparion[43]—is a traditional one. The picture given by theologians like Moltmann and Jüngel is even more startling, for here we must think of God taking death into the divine life and becoming part of God's experience. While we should not speak in a simplistic way of a "death of God" (as if God just ceased to exist on Good Friday), the cross means that we must be able to speak of "death in God."[44]

The importance of the cross for our theme of atonement will be dealt with in detail in following chapters. We should, however, proceed systematically with the implications of a theology of the Crucified One. We begin by removing a misapprehension about this theology, and then discuss our knowledge of God and God's relationship with the world.

The Crucified Christ is Risen

It would be easy to get the impression that a theology which focuses on the cross must be grim and life-despising. But it is essential to remember the fundamental Easter proclamation that "Jesus of Nazareth, who was crucified . . . has been raised" (Mark 16:6). Cross and resurrection must go together if the Christian message is not to be distorted. If Jesus had not been raised then we would know nothing about his crucifixion. He would be just one more nameless victim of Roman imperial power.

On the other hand, resurrection must not be proclaimed without the cross. That is one of the crudest forms of a theology of glory, one which is present in all too many Easter celebrations. The Risen One bears the marks of crucifixion—the point made by Luke 24:39 and John 20:20, however we may think of the accuracy of historical details in the resurrection narratives. (Pascal speculated that Christ allowed only his wounds to be touched after the resurrection.[45]) The cross does not get rid of what Paul called the *skandalon* of the cross. It even intensifies that scandal because it means that the one in whom people are called to put their trust and who is worshipped in the Christian community is the Crucified One.[46] This scandal has not just a human dimension but a cosmic one. As Irenaeus put it, "The Son of God was crucified for all and for everything, having traced the sign of the cross on all things."[47]

This means that when we speak of the cross we should also have the resurrection in mind, and when we proclaim the resurrection it must be the resurrection of the Crucified One. In many cases "the cross" should be understood as a kind of theological shorthand for "the cross-resurrection event."

The resurrection of Jesus means that God continues to give permanent value to the world which he has created. It is remarkable that some modern theologians who claim to have great respect for the natural sciences hold some type of spiritualized view of the resurrection which does not, for example, require the tomb of Jesus to be empty. The implication of such a view is that the physical world which the natural sciences study is not really very important.[48] An understanding of Easter as the raising of Jesus in his body-soul-spirit-mind totality keeps us from such a fate. Paul speaks in 1 Corinthians 15:35-55 of the resurrection as transformation: "It is sown a physical body, it is raised a spiritual body" (verse 44)—yet a body.

The resurrection of Jesus means that human sin cannot finally overcome the purpose of God for the world. It is a sign that creation is to be transformed and will not end in futility. It is more than just a sign, however, because it is the beginning of the actual transformation from death to life: Christ is "the first fruits of those who have died" (1 Corinthians 15:20). The cross-resurrection event is the turning point in the history of creation. And the resurrection is those things because—and only because—it is the resurrection of the crucified.

The Cross Reveals the True God

A theology of the cross looks to the cross-resurrection event as the primary source of our knowledge of God. This is what Luther means by saying that "true theology and recognition of God are in the crucified Christ."[49] We are to begin with what God has revealed of the divine character in the event of the crucifixion of Jesus of Nazareth and the resurrection of the Crucified One. Luther makes that claim as part of his argument for Heidelberg Thesis 20: "That person deserves to be called a theologian, however, who comprehends the visible and manifest things of God seen through suffering and the cross."

That is the antithesis of the previous Thesis 19: "That person does not deserve to be called a theologian who looks upon the invisible things of God as though they were clearly perceptible in those things that have actually happened (or have been made, created.")[50] With this we renounce the idea that some natural knowledge of God derived from general experience of the world and human reason, independent of revelation, can give us a natural theology to serve as a foundation for specifically Christian theology.

But does not Romans 1:18-20 speak of a knowledge of God that is evident in the natural world? That is a common argument but it fails to see what Paul's is doing there. The apostle does indeed says that such evidence is available in the world, but his point is that people uniformly distort it and create idols. They may think that there is "a God," but sin keeps them from knowing anything about who that God is. Thus this supposed natural knowledge of God inevitably leads to bad theology or something that is not really theology at all. That is the point that Luther is making in Thesis 19, for the Latin of that thesis.[51]

The statement that the cross is God's fundamental revelation should not be understood too narrowly. It is not only the events of Good Friday, circa. A.D. 30, that tell us anything about God. Scripture from Genesis to Revelation bears witness to God's historical revelation which culminates in Christ. The biblical story, as a whole and in its parts, can be seen to have a cruciform shape, a pattern of death and resurrection.[52]

In particular, the life of Christ as well as his death has this shape. The hymn which Paul quotes in Philippians 2:5-11 tells of one "who, though he was in the form of God . . . emptied himself [*heauton ekenosen*], taking the form of a slave, being born in human likeness. And being found in human form, he humbled himself and became obedient to the point of death—even death on a cross." A double descent is described here. The Son of God "emptied himself," limited himself to the condition of a creature. And he became human not as one of "the great ones of the earth" (2 Samuel 7:9), but as an itinerant teacher who washed his disciples' feet.

Christ's emptying—his *kenosis*—and humbling were not mere tactics used to accomplish some goal, but to give profound insight into God. As Gordon Fee puts it in his commentary on this text, "For in 'pouring himself out' and 'humbling himself to death on the cross' Christ Jesus has revealed the character of God himself."[53] This means that we should not be surprised to find that God chooses to limit Godself not only in the incarnation but in other aspects of the divine involvement with the world.

Since authors mean different things when they use the concept of *kenosis*, it is important to be clear about the sense in which it will be used here. *Kenosis* is not nihilism and, while it might offer a point of contact with Buddhism, it is not the concept of "emptiness" found in that tradition. It does not mean the absence or inactivity of God but rather divine self-limitation. The same Paul who spoke of the emptying of the Son of God in the incarnation also wrote that "in Christ God was reconciling the world to himself" (2 Corinthians 5:19). I will argue in the following sections that God inspired the biblical writers and is continually working in the world, but that these actions have the same kenotic character. God normally does not act in ways that are beyond the capacities of the instruments God uses.

The fact that we know God first from God's revelation in the history of Israel which culminates in Christ does not mean that our knowledge of the natural world can contribute nothing to theology or that there is no legitimate natural theology. But scientific knowledge of the world must be viewed in the light of God's revelation in Christ in order to have theological significance and provide a valid natural theology, as Thomas Torrance emphasized.[54] This can be called a dependent natural theology, in contrast to natural theologies which are independent of revelation. The term "theology of nature" is used for similar concepts by other authors, but that language blurs the necessary distinction. A theology of nature deals with the theological significance of the natural world itself, while a natural theology, in the accepted meaning of the term, deals with what can be said theologically on the basis of what is known about the natural world. Any attempt to develop an adequate understanding of creation will involve some type of "theology of nature" and some theologies of this type may eschew any appeal to God's historical revelation.

The Biblical Witness to the God Revealed by the Cross

Our access to God's revelatory acts in history is through the scriptures, the inspired witness to those acts. One of the issues that has to be dealt with in serious science-theology dialogue is the tension between, on the one hand, the Christian claim that the biblical writings are indeed trustworthy and authoritative witnesses to revelation and, on the other hand, well-established scientific knowledge that conflicts with some of the statements about the world in those writings.

We encounter these tensions already in the Bible's first creation account, Genesis 1:1—2:4a. First, scientific investigation has made it quite certain that the universe, including the earth and all its living things, did not come into being in a single six-day period. The beginning of cosmic expansion can be dated to about 13.7 billion years ago, the earth was formed about 4.5 billion years in the past, terrestrial life began within a billion years after that, and anatomically modern humans came into being more than a hundred thousand years ago.

We do not really know whether or not the authors and redactors of Genesis actually thought that the world was created in six literal days. Their primary purpose was not to give chronological information but to convey the belief that the God of Israel is the creator of all things, including humanity, and God has certain purposes for creation. We might give them the benefit of the doubt on the question of whether they were concerned with questions about when and how long. In the seventeenth century Pascal, who knew something of both science and theology, argued as follows:

> [A]ccording to St. Augustine and St. Thomas, when we meet with a passage even in the Scripture, the literal meaning of which, at first sight, appears contrary to what the senses or reason are certainly persuaded of, we must not attempt to reject their testimony in this case, and yield them up to the authority of that apparent sense of the Scripture, but we must interpret the Scripture, and seek out therein another sense agreeable to that sensible truth; because, the Word of God being infallible in the facts which it records, and the information of the senses and of reason, acting in their sphere, being certain also, it follows that there must be an agreement between these two sources of knowledge. And as Scripture may be interpreted in different ways, whereas the testimony of the senses is uniform, we must in these matters adopt as the true interpretation of Scripture that view which corresponds with the faithful report of the senses.[55]

The argument is even stronger if we do not hold that scripture is "infallible in the facts which it records." We should refrain from insisting on the literal sense of texts against clear scientific evidence. We should also resist the temptation to read into texts modern scientific meanings, as is done, for example, by those think they can find references to the big bang in Genesis 1.

It is understandable if today's readers wonder why a supposedly inspired account of the creation of the world couldn't be closer to what we know today really happened. The question is sharpened if we realize that within the creation narrative—understood as literal history or not—the world is pictured in the way that people of the ancient near east understood it, a way that in some of its features is obsolete. The sky is described in Genesis 1:6-7 as a "dome" (NRSV) or "firmament" (KJV), a solid structure. Above that dome there was a cosmic ocean: "the waters that were above the dome" that come down as rain when "the windows of the heavens" are opened (Genesis 7:11) and that were still supposed to be in place when Psalm 148:4 was written.[56] Modern astronomy and meteorology have long realized that this is not the way the world is.

It is often said, and of course it is true, that the Bible is not a textbook of science. Its purpose is to speak about God's relationship with the world and God's will for our lives. But it has descriptions of the world and its history that its writers clearly thought were true but simply are not! If it means anything to say that scripture is inspired, why couldn't God manage to make it more accurate? Nobody expects up-to-date technical accounts of astrophysics or paleontology, but why couldn't God have inspired an elementary description of a cosmic explosion and gradual development of living things instead of what we have in Genesis?

There is a long history of Christian discussion of what can be meant by the inspiration of scripture.[57] It is surely more subtle than God putting words into a writer's brain. In the present situation the concept of *kenosis* is germane. Presumably God could indeed have moved biblical writers and redactors to give elementary descriptions of the big bang, evolution, the nature of the sky, and the hydrological cycle. But that isn't how knowledge of the world developed in the cultures of the ancient near east, and if the Holy Spirit acted within the limits of human knowledge about the world, the cosmologies of those cultures—which are now outdated—would provide the language in which biblical statements about creation would be expressed.

The idea of "accommodation" or "condescension" in the inspiration of scripture goes back to some church fathers and was used, for example, by Calvin.[58] We need to realize, however, that this cannot just mean that the biblical writers accommodated their words to the state of knowledge of their contemporaries. It is *God* who accommodates the divine message to the limitations of human culture, including those of the writers themselves, being willing to use even views that would turn out to be wrong. But though there is scientific *error* in the Bible (e.g., a dome over the earth) there is no intent to *deceive*. It is even a blessing that the Bible does not freeze scientific understanding of the world at any stage of development, that of the first millennium B.C., the time of Newton, or today.

An analogy has often been drawn between the inspiration of scripture and the incarnation.[59] Just as Christ is both fully human and fully divine, the Bible is both a collection of human writings and the Word of God. When we remember that the incarnation includes the divine *kenosis* we will be able to see that the scientific limitations of scripture are not embarrassments which must be explained away, but are rather a consequence of the fullness with which God enters into the history of our world in the activity of revelation. [60]

We will also see that scientific knowledge of evolution challenges some aspects of traditional theological anthropologies. Paul's statements that "death came through a human being" and "all die in Adam" (1 Corinthians 15:21-22) involve more than death as a biological phenomenon, as we will discuss in Chapter IV. But it seems clear that Paul did think that physical death originated with a sin of the first humans, an idea that now seems quite implausible. At one level we can simply say "Paul was wrong," but we should not leave it at that. Paul's belief made sense in the context of the Jewish culture in which he grew up and was educated, and the Holy Spirit accommodated what was said about the significance of Christ to that belief, mistaken though it was as a matter of biology. There is, however, more to our concept of death than biology alone, and we will consider its broader meaning when we discuss human sin and divine reconciliation.

While we need to recognize that the biblical authors put some mistaken ideas about the world into their writings, we also have to consider the possibility that through the Spirit's inspiration there was, in some cases, more truth in what those human authors wrote than they realized. Many Israelites, as well as the whole nation, had suffered and died, and there is no reason to think that the writer of the fourth servant song of Isaiah (52:13—53:12) had conscious knowledge of the passion of the specific Israelite Jesus of Nazareth several hundred years in the future. But it certainly is providential that the text speaks so clearly of the significance of his suffering and death. Similarly, we need to be open to the possibility that the Holy Spirit used the mythic material from the cultures of the writers of early Genesis to convey some theological truth about the beginnings of the human race. This old idea of a "fuller sense" (*sensus plenior*) of scripture is not thought of highly by modern critical scholars, but we should not discount the ingenuity of the Holy Spirit in working within cultural limitations.[61]

Creation Bears the Mark of the Cross

Several New Testament texts speak of Christ as the agent of creation. "All things came into being through" the Word (John 1:3), and "all things have been created through him and for him . . . and in him all things hold together" (Colossians 1:16-17).

1 Corinthians 8:6 and Hebrews 1:2 are also relevant here. When we read the Old Testament in the light of the New Testament, passages which speak of the role of God's Word or Wisdom in creation, such as Psalm 33:6 and Proverbs 8:22-31, are drawn into the discussion. The Colossians text in particular reminds us that creation is not limited to origination. All things also "hold together" in Christ and have been created "for him."

Creation is a work of the Trinity, not of just one of the trinitarian persons, and a theology of the Crucified One points us to an important feature of this trinitarian work. The key to this understanding, the concept of *kenosis*, has been important in recent discussions of divine action and its relationship with scientific understanding of natural processes.[62]

Science discerns a tremendous degree of regularity in the natural world, and the ways in which particular kinds of entities—especially at the level of fundamental fields and particles—behave imply a close linkage between what they are and what they do. This suggests that God does not simply move passive objects around in arbitrary ways, but that creatures are real causes of phenomena. We can best understand God's action in cooperation with created agents when we consider a human worker using a machine to accomplish some task. In scholastic language, the First Cause acts through secondary causes.

The regularity of natural processes also indicates that God limits divine action to be in accord with the laws—themselves God's creation—that created agents obey. (What we call "the laws of physics" are only approximations to the true laws or patterns of the world.) That is quite understandable if *kenosis* characterizes the way in which God acts in the universe. Because of this kenotic aspect of divine action, what happens in the world can be described scientifically in terms of natural processes obeying rational laws, with no reference to God required. God's presence and action in the world is thus hidden, as God is hidden in the God-forsakenness of Calvary and is perceived only by faith in the Crucified One. This is, nevertheless, a gift because it means that we can understand our world on its own terms and have some control over what takes place in it.

Some authors have argued that this concept of *kenosis* is relevant only for soteriology and should not be extended to creation,[63] but such a restriction is not possible if we hold that the cross-resurrection event is the fundamental revelation of the true God. As Fee put it in a statement that was quoted earlier, Christ's soteriological *kenosis* "revealed the character of God himself," [64] the same God who is at work in creation.

Kenosis cannot stand by itself as a model of how God works in the world because it tells us what God does *not* do rather than what God does. God does not operate with creatures in arbitrary ways that exceed their natural capacities but cooperates with creatures, using them as instruments but respecting the dynamic features with which he has endowed them. As we already pointed out, however, this negative character of *kenosis* does not mean that God is absent or inactive in some processes of the world. God is "almighty" in the classical sense of being the ultimate cause of everything that happens, but God does that while respecting the integrity of creation.

The way in which humans work with tools provides an obvious model for God's cooperation with creatures. But while this model is helpful, it should not lure us into treating interactions between God and creatures as if they were relations between two entities within the world. To search for what is sometimes referred to as the "causal joint" suggests that the problem of divine action is like a scientist's attempt to find a mathematical expression that describes the interaction between two physical systems like an electromagnetic field and a charged particle. But God is not a being within the world on the same ontological level as photons and electrons, and theology is not physics. We observe and measure the ways in which fields and particles influence one another by means of our senses and our physical instruments. We "see" God at work in the world when we place such phenomena in the context of Christian faith.

To say this in another, and more traditional, way: Our model of divine action is an analogy, not a straightforward description. It is an attempt to maintain the belief that God is indeed omnipotent while also insisting that creatures really do things in the world. And no apology need be made for the analogical character of this model. All such attempts to describe divine action (like language about God "luring" the world forward in some versions of process theology) have similar limitations.

God's creative activity through the evolutionary process is of special importance for discussions of atonement, for it has some critical implications for theological anthropology. In one sense evolution is "just" another application of the view of divine action which has been set out here. God cooperates with natural processes at the microscopic level, including the development, replication, and mutation of DNA, and at the macroscopic level, including environmental changes, natural selection, and the emergence of new species. The idea that God acts through such an apparently amoral and cruel process as natural selection is responsible for much of the religious opposition to evolution. Chiasmic cosmology does not try to minimize the harsh aspects of evolution but insists that the one who creates in this way is also the one who becomes a participant and fellow-sufferer in the evolutionary process, getting killed in the "struggle for survival."[65]

Since we will be speaking about salvation as God's work of new creation, it will be natural to ask if there are parallels between that work and the "ordinary" divine activity of creation. As we will see, there are such parallels but there are also differences which we will have to maintain if we are to avoid a crudely physical model of atonement.

Our discussion of sin and salvation will also require us to say more about evolution, and human evolution in particular, than the generality that evolution is God's way of creating. We turn to that more detailed treatment in the next two chapters when we consider what God intends for humans to be and what we in fact are.

The Cross and God's Purpose for Creation

The view of divine action sketched in the previous section cannot be supported by observational evidence in the same way that theories in the natural sciences can be. The fact that God generally acts in a hidden way in the world means that science can describe what goes on in the world "though God were not given," as Bonhoeffer said in one of his prison letters.[66] And this means that those who wish to do so can reject the idea that God acts through natural processes as an unnecessary additions to scientific explanations. They do not, as Laplace is supposed to have said to Napoleon, "need that hypothesis."[67]

Science can give very good accounts of what takes place in the world. The situation is quite different if we ask about the purpose of what goes on in the world. Since the demise of the Aristotelian approach to physics, scientists have been wary of admitting a purpose for the natural world into their theories. Steven Weinberg's statement about the lack of any "point" to the universe that was quoted earlier is typical in this regard. But it is one thing to say that science cannot discern any point to the world and quite another to assert that there simply is no point or purpose.

Theologians, of course, have talked about God's purpose or purposes for the world, but a great deal of what has been said could be dismissed by nonbelievers for the same reason that statements about divine action can be rejected. Divorced from their grounding in Christian faith, these theological assertions seem to be arbitrary additions to a scientific description of the world. The biblical claim that through the growth of plants the God of Israel provides bread and wine for humanity (Psalm 104:14-15) seems no more plausible than the idea that Ceres and Bacchus provide those things.

Things are different if we look at the world in the context of a theology of the cross. This provides a unified picture of divine action in the world *and* of divine purpose for the world that takes science seriously.[68] God acts in the world in a way that is consistent with the divine revelation in the event of the cross, and God's purpose for creation is to unite all things with the crucified and risen Christ. As Barth put it:[69]

> The world came into being, it was created and sustained by the little child that was born on Bethlehem, by the Man who died on the Cross of Golgotha, and the third day rose again. *That* is the Word of creation, by which all things were brought into being. That is where the *meaning* of creation comes from, and that is why it says at the beginning of the Bible: "In the beginning God made heaven and earth, and God said, 'Let there be. . .'"."

Of course the coherence of these two aspects of our theology does not prove that that theology is correct in the sense that scientific descriptions can be. But it does suggest that theology can help to make sense of the understanding of the world that science gives us.

THE HUMAN CREATURE

The Creation of Humankind

In order to discuss salvation adequately, we need to have some understanding of what creation is saved for and what it is saved from. Since God's saving work begins within and for humanity in the human Jesus Christ, our treatment will begin there as well. In this chapter we consider what it means to speak of humankind as God's creation— how we came into being and what God intended for us to be. The next chapter will discuss what in fact has become of us.

The Bible's statements about creation are not exhausted by its first two chapters. Old Testament texts such as Psalm 104 and Isaiah 40:21-28 should also be noted, and we have already referred to some passages in the New Testament that are important in this connection. But for our purposes it will be best to begin with Genesis 1:1-2:4a and 2:4b-25, in both of which humans have a prominent place. Human beings have a prominent place in both of the creation stories, Genesis 1:1-2:4a and 2:4b-25. In the first account, after other living things have been created, God deliberates and determines to make humankind (*'adham*) "in our image, according to our likeness" (verse 26). So "male and female he created them" and told them to "have dominion over the fish of the sea and over the birds of the air and over every living thing that moves upon the face of the earth" (verses 27-28). Made in the divine image, humans are to rule the world as God's representatives, according to the example of their creator.

In the second account, on the other hand, the importance of the human is brought out by placing its creation at the beginning of the story. Now the creator does not simply speak something into being but literally gets down in the dirt to form the human—again *'adham*. Here we see the meaning of that term: *'adham* is from *'adhamah*, ground, since taken "from the dust of the ground." God "breathed into his nostrils the breath of life, and the man became a living be- ing;" (2:7). Then he is placed in God's garden to "serve" and to "guard" it —more accurate translations of the Hebrew words than the tradi- tional "till" and "keep" in 2:15.[70] This commission and the naming of the animals (formed, like the human, from the ground) in verses 19- 20 correspond to the command to "have dominion" in the first account. But this creation story is not complete until the woman is formed from the man's side and, in the picture of a primal wedding, brought to him (verses 21-25).

Speaking of "correspondence" between the two accounts does not mean that they are really saying just the same things or that they are two parts of a single narrative. There is an overarching theologi- cal unity, but the fact that matters are spoken of in different ways is also significant.

While humanity has important and honored roles in both accounts, there are also some things which tradition may have led us to expect but which are in fact absent. Humans are not pictured as in any sense "perfect." They are not said to have tremendous wisdom, great physi- cal beauty, immunity from disease, immortality, or any of the other extraordinary qualities that have sometimes been read into the texts. The commissions given to the humans imply that they are able to obey and have mental capacities and skills needed to carry out their tasks, or at least the potential to develop such abilities. But these implied qualities fall far short of the idea of the English bishop Rob- ert South that "An Aristotle was but the rubbish of an Adam."[71]

Secondly, humanity is not itself the end of God's creative work. The formation of humankind as the sixth day's last act in the first account is followed by the seventh day, the Sabbath. In the Jewish tradition this came to be celebrated as a type of the Kingdom of God, the final and complete establishing of God's reign. (This is why so many of Jesus' healings are placed by the gospels on the Sabbath, the right time for the messianic signs of the inbreaking of the Kingdom of God—cf. Isaiah 35:5-6.[72]) Thus the formation of all things is from the beginning oriented toward the eschatological reign of God.

The picture is rather different in the second account. This does end with humanity, but not as a collection of independent humans. "The Lord God in his goodness created us male and female, and by the gift of marriage founded human community" is the way one mar- riage service puts it.[73] A harmonious society, not Hobbes' "war of all against all," is God's intention. Creation of the animals as a preliminary but inadequate step in this direction even hints at an extension of this community beyond the bounds of humankind.

This is a description—a theological rather than an historical one—of humanity without sin. "The man and his wife were both naked, and were not ashamed" (verse 25). As we will see in the next chapter, what we know of evolution suggests that human sin was in a sense inevitable, but God did not create humans as sinners.

We cannot be certain whether or not the writer of Genesis 2—3 thought of "the man" and "the woman" as historical persons. The point in Genesis at which 'adham is to be understood as a proper name, "Adam," is debated.[74] Adam as the first man is listed in genealogies (Genesis 5:1-5, 1 Chronicles 1:1, and Luke 3:38) and may be referred to in Hosea 6:7.[75] But Adam as an individual and the story in Genesis 2—3 is never mentioned in the Old Testament's recitations of God's saving acts in history. This suggests that when those texts were set down, Israel did not see him as an historical figure.[76]

This changed in the intertestamental period. "The first-formed father of the world" and "his transgression" are at the beginning of a resume of the biblical history in Wisdom 10:1, written probably around 100 B.C. Thus Paul shared what was apparently a common Jewish view of his contemporaries when he wrote about Adam as an historical person. We will deal further with that in the next chapter.

These opening chapters of Genesis are important, but a number of other biblical texts deal with creation. We will not discuss them all, but at this point we call attention to two passages in the New Testament. In the Christ hymn of Colossians 1:15-20 we read:

> He is the image of the invisible God, the firstborn of all creation; for in him all things in heaven and on earth were created, things visible and invisible, whether thrones or dominions or rulers or powers—all things have been created through him and for him. He himself is before all things, and in him all things hold together. He is the head of the body, the church; he is the beginning, the firstborn from the dead, so that he might come to have first place in everything. For in him all the fullness of God was pleased to dwell, and through him God was pleased to reconcile to himself all things, whether on earth or in heaven, by making peace through the blood of his cross.

The subject of this hymn is the incarnate Christ, not the "unfleshed Word," as reference to "the blood of his cross" makes clear. That will be important when we discuss the cosmic scope of atonement, but at this point we want to emphasize that Christ is not only the agent of creation ("through him") but also its goal ('for him'). This suggests that God's purpose for creation is the uniting of "all things" with God Incarnate. This is made explicit in Ephesians 1:8b-10:

> With all wisdom and insight he [God] has made known to us the mystery of his will, according to his good pleasure that he set forth in Christ, as a plan for the fullness of time, to gather up all things in him, things in heaven and things on earth.

The incarnation, then, was not simply a means that God devised to solve the problem posed by human sin. Logically it precedes human sinfulness and even the creation of the world. God made a world in which a suitable flesh could evolve in which God would take flesh. That this has not been the majority view throughout Christian history is shown by the fact that Anselm could pose the question about the need for atonement as one about the reason for the incarnation: *Cur deus homo*? Some medieval theologians, such as Albert the Great and Duns Scotus, did think that the incarnation would have taken place even if humanity had not sinned. The influential answer of Aquinas to the question "Whether, If Man Had Not Sinned, God Would Have Become Incarnate?" was, however, in the negative.[77]

Barth's view, which we noted at the end of the last chapter, was a significant factor in a shift in more recent theological opinion toward the belief that the incarnation was God's intention from the beginning. While it is true that, as the Nicene Creed says, "for us and for our salvation he came down from heaven," the texts quoted above from Colossians and Ephesians indicate that this was not just God's "Plan B."

But of course the incarnation was not realized at the beginning of creation. Or, to use other biblical images, God's perfect reign was not established at the world's origin, and "a sabbath rest still remains for the people of God" (Hebrews 4:9). One of the more misleading ideas about the doctrine of creation is that God made a perfect world in the beginning. If that had been the case then God's intention must have been that the world remain unchanged in its static perfection—for what is perfect can change only by becoming less perfect! Just the command to "be fruitful and multiply" shows that that is not what scripture envisions.

"The world was made, not in time, but simultaneously with time" said Augustine.[78] Time, change, and history are aspects of the universe which God intended in creating it. God created a universe that was to develop toward its divinely intended goal. Creation is a dynamic process rather than a static order of being.

This means, among other things, that we should not expect to learn what God intends for humans only from Genesis 1 and 2. These chapters give us very little information by way of a pattern for what humans are supposed to be. The biblical model for that is not the "first Adam" but the "last" (1 Corinthians 15:45), Jesus Christ. It is Jesus who shows us humanity as God intends it. Thus we are told in Ephesians 4:13 that we are to come "to maturity, to the measure of the full stature of Christ."

With the benefit of hindsight we can see here an opening for an "evolutionary" understanding of humankind. This does not mean, however, that the Bible itself "teaches evolution" in the sense of today's scientific theories. It should be no surprise, in view of our discussion of the *kenotic* character of the inspiration of scripture, that it does not. People of ancient near-eastern cultures did not have a modern scientific understanding of paleontology or genetics, so the creation accounts of Israel say nothing about these things. In order to have an adequate understanding of humanity we need to place today's scientific knowledge in the context of the theology sketched in the previous chapter.

The Science of Human Origins

We do not know the details of human evolution as well as we would like, but that is in part because we are naturally more interested in our own history than in that of some species of tree or insect. For our purposes a broad view will suffice. To begin with, we have a fairly good understanding of how evolution in general works.[79] The mechanism of natural selection which Darwin and Wallace proposed in 1858 is the major thing that drives the process.[80] There will be variations among members of any species, and in any particular environment some members will, therefore, be more likely to survive and produce offspring to which they will pass on their traits. The accumulation of favorable variations may eventually lead to organisms sufficiently different from ancestral types that they will be unable to interbreed with them. This means that a new species has arisen.

What Darwin and Wallace did not know was the mechanism of transmission of genetic information from one generation to the next. Mendel's work and his proposal of particulate "factors"—what we now call genes—appeared a few years after Darwin and Wallace's first publications but in an obscure journal, so that it was almost completely unknown for over thirty years. Discovery of Mendel's work made it possible to begin to understand the variations which play such an important role in the theories of Darwin and Wallace. The discovery of the location of genes along the chromosomes of cells, their composition of DNA and the double helix structure of that molecule, and the genetic code—all of the work of the twentieth century in molecular genetics—has had a major impact on our understanding of evolutionary processes.

We came into being, like all life on earth, though an evolutionary process that began at least 3.5 billion years ago. Sequencing of the genomes of our own species, *Homo sapiens*, and of other species has shown surprisingly close agreement. We have sequences of DNA that are found in bacteria and houseflies more genetic agreement with other mammals such as mice, and most of all with the great apes.[81] These genetic correlations and the fact that our genetic code (the "language" in which DNA directs the functioning of cellular machinery) is the same as that of other terrestrial organisms strongly suggests that we all share a common origin and are parts of the same evolutionary process.

The extent to which two species' DNA correspond is an indication of how closely they are related. By this criterion we are distantly related to flies, closer to mice, and closest of all extant species to chimpanzees, followed by the other great apes. This agrees with the evolutionary pattern suggested by gross anatomy and other considerations. (Linnaeus had already classified humans among the primates in the eighteenth century.) We have not descended from modern apes, but they are our closest living relatives—our "cousins," to put it loosely. This means that the behavior of present-day apes will probably be a better guide for us in understanding the behaviors of our pre-human ancestors than would be the behaviors of other extant species.

Present estimates are that our hominid family of the primates shared its last common ancestor with the pongids—represented by today's great apes—around seven million years ago. Older fossil remains dated after this split are classified in the genus *Ardepithecus*, then *Australopithecus*, and most recently *Homo*. There are a number of species in each genus and the precise evolutionary connections are debated by paleoanthropologists. Ardepithecine and australopithecine fossils are found only in Africa, but those of homo are also found in Asia, the Middle East and Europe. Our immediate ancestor was most likely *Homo erectus*, whose remains were first found in Indonesia ("Java man") and China ("Peking man"—one of the subjects of research by Teilhard de Chardin, whose theological ideas we will meet later[82]). The picture is far from complete, as the recent discovery of the controversial "hobbits," *Homo floresiensis,* and ongoing debates about relationships between our species and Neanderthals show.

Certainly hominids originated in Africa, but the birthplace of our own species, *Homo sapiens*, is still debated.[83] Proponents of the widely accepted "out of Africa" scenario argue that genetic data and cultural artifacts indicate that around 125,000 years ago a population of anatomically modern humans left Africa and spread throughout the world, supplanting earlier populations of *Homo erectus* and the Neanderthals whose ancestors had themselves emigrated from Africa considerably earlier. The "multiregional continuity" model, on the other hand, sees present human populations in different parts of the world as being descended from groups that had already existed in Africa, Asia, and Europe, the latter two sites as a result of earlier migrations from Africa. Models that combine some features of both scenarios have also been proposed.

"Out of Africa" gives the closest approximation to the traditional theological view that humanity had a single place of origin. This is not, however, essential for the models of sin and atonement that I will be suggesting. Moreover, as we will discuss in the next section, we need not assume that humanity in a theological sense is identical with our biological species. Thus we do not have to choose one or the other of the scientific theories about the origin of anatomically modern humans in order to proceed theologically.

What Are Human Beings?

In the context of Psalm 8, this question in verse 4 is rhetorical: Humans seem so insignificant in comparison with the heavens, yet God has given them such a position of honor! The only humans the psalmist, like the authors of the Genesis creation stories, knew were members of the species *Homo sapiens*. But now that we have learned that God created humanity through a slow evolutionary process rather than in a single event, real questions about who qualifies as "human" naturally arise. Were Neanderthals human? What about *Homo erectus?* The biblical writers didn't know about them but if they had, would they have considered them *'adham*?[84]

For science as well, a general quality that we might call "humanness" is not necessarily limited to members of our species.[85] The arguments of evolutionary paleobiologist Simon Conway Morris are of interest here.[86] He describes the widespread phenomenon of convergence, the tendency of differing evolutionary paths to reach similar ways of meeting similar needs. Features often seen as distinctively human, such as "giant brains, tool use, bipedality, and even a precision grip"[87] are found in other terrestrial species. Thus he suggests that if life does exist on other planets (which he considers quite improbable) evolution there is likely to have given rise to species that have many of the general features of "humanness" that we possess. But while biological considerations may inform our thinking, our fundamental concern is with what it means to be human in a theological sense.

As we saw earlier, the most basic reply to that question is that Jesus Christ is the pattern of true humanity into which we are supposed to "grow up" (Ephesians 4:15). The answer to the psalmist's question "What are human beings?" is given in the New Testament. The writer of the Letter to the Hebrews quotes the psalm's statement about God "subjecting" all things to the human, and observes that "we do not yet see everything in subjection to him." "But," the argument continues, "We do see Jesus" (Hebrews 2:6-9 RSV). Christ is what God was aiming for.

Having said that, we need to go back and fill in some details. In order to make any correlation between scientific and theological understandings we need to ask about the observable features which would make it possible for creatures to correspond to the way in which scripture describes human beings.

In both of the creation stories humans are distinguished from other animals by the fact that God communicates with them. While neither of the Genesis stories is an historical account of some primordial revelation, the rest of the biblical story only makes sense if at some point there was some such revelation – that God made himself known, however dimly, to hominids at some epoch of evolutionary history. Paul says in the first part of Romans 1:20 that "Ever since the creation of the world his [God's] eternal power and divine nature, invisible though they are, have been understood and seen through the things he has made." I argued in the previous chapter that it is a mistake to appeal to this verse in support of an independent natural theology because of the problem of sin. Paul's point in verses 19-31 is that people distort any knowledge of God in nature and create idols. The only function of the knowledge that Paul speaks of is, to complete verse 20, "so they are without excuse." But that would not have been the case before humans had sinned. In fact, precisely an original distortion of this knowledge of God could be seen as the beginning of sin!

At what epoch some hominids may have been made aware of God we just do not know. But we cannot simply assume that this corresponded to the emergence of *Homo sapiens* or "anatomically modern humans." Those modern categories are not necessarily identical with the theological concept of *'adham*.

In both of the Genesis texts, and in different ways, God commissions humankind to care for the earth —to "have dominion" as God's representative and to "serve and guard" God's garden. That implies that God has made them able to understand the command and has given them the intelligence and skill to carry it out – or at least the potential to do so. In the words of one of the church's eucharistic prayers, God "blessed us with memory, reason, and skill."[88]

The concern that some Christians will feel about our inability to pin down just when humankind in a theological sense came into being may be due to a tacit assumption that we are the only really important part of the creation story, and that a sharp boundary must be drawn between humanity and the rest of the living world. But scripture denies this assumption—from the picture of God caring for the beasts of the wilderness in Job 39 to the sweeping statements about God's purpose for "all things" in Ephesians and Colossians. And from the scientific side, the sciences of ecology and evolution have shown us how inextricably we are connected with all life on earth,

If these considerations move us to ask, "How then can we locate Adam and Eve in the course of evolution?" the blunt answer must be, "We probably cannot." In fact, the assumption underlying the question should be dropped, for our current genetic knowledge makes it extremely unlikely that present day humans can be traced back to a single couple at some point in earth's history. There was at one point a genetic "bottleneck," a relatively small population of a few thousand people who are our ancestors. But that initial population could not have been just a single male and a single female.[89]

A couple of lines of argument are relevant here.[90]   We have fairly good estimates of the rate at which mutations, changes in DNA, take place. Over many generations, an ancestor's two versions of a gene (alleles) will diversify among his or her descendants. We can use the variety of alleles as a molecular clock to estimate the length of time that has elapsed between present day species and their ancestors. This can be done with the variety of human histocompatibility alleles (crucial for the functioning of our immune systems) in the world today. The result is that it would require between five and ten million years for the present diversity to evolve from a single male-female couple. Unless we want to consider "Adam and Eve" to be the ancestors not only of hominids but perhaps even of modern apes, we have to conclude that not all humans today are descendants from a single male-female pair.

It is also possible, by comparing the human genome with that of chimpanzees and gorillas, and also by examining variations within the human genome alone. To estimate the minimum population of *Homo sapiens* that has ever existed. The result is that there must have been at least a few thousand such humans at any time since they emerged as a separate species.

It is important to emphasize that the theological model of early humanity that will be proposed here does not depend on the number of hominids to be considered the first humans or on when they came into being. The model would not have to be changed in any essential way if it were possible to understand our species to have a single ancestral couple. But it is best to be realistic about the fact that this now seems quite unlikely. Obviously this raises questions about the ways in which Paul uses the figure of "Adam" in Romans 5 and 1 Corinthians 15. We will address those questions in the next chapter.

Mortality

One inescapable feature of humanity today is that, sooner or later, we all die. That is an aspect of the way the world is. The scientific evidence for the dying of animals not only today but before the advent of humanity is overwhelming. Physical death is part of the natural order in which we are embedded, and is even one of the forces that drives evolution. In an important sense we are here because of death, which must, then, be seen as part of the means by which God has created us.

But the idea of "death before the fall" is very troublesome for some Christians. Historian of science Edward Davis has suggested that refusal to accept it is the primary motive for rejection of evolution and acceptance of "young earth creationism" for many Christians.[91]

A popular literal understanding of Genesis is that there was no death at all in the world before Adam and Eve sinned in the Garden of Eden. That extreme view has no basis in either theology or science. Biblical texts that connect sin and death, Genesis 3:19, Romans 5:12-21 and 1 Corinthians 15:21-22, refer to humanity, and there is no reason to insist that they include other animals. In the last analysis, the rejection of "death before the fall" rests on the belief that God created an originally perfect world in which all destructive processes were absent. The Bible itself simply does not say this. Those who realize that God was willing himself to enter into death in order to bring creation to fulfillment will have less trouble with the idea that God made a world in which creatures would die.

What about human death? There is no scientific reason to distinguish between humanity and other animals as far as biological death is concerned. "In the day that you eat of it you shall surely die" (Genesis 2:17 NKJV) is spoken to the human, and this can be taken to mean that if he does not eat, he will not die. But this verse should not be understood literally, for when the man does later eat of the tree, he does not die on the same day. That suggests that more than simple physical death is in view here.

One can, of course appeal to Psalm 90:4 and 2 Peter 3:8 and argue that the deaths of Adam and the other antediluvian patriarchs before they reached the age of one thousand years means that they died within "a day." Some of the church fathers did just that.[92] But those texts that speak of a thousand years in God's sight being like a day and, in 2 Peter, a day being like a thousand years are clearly meant to contrast God's enduring character with the ephemeral lives of humans, not to set up a precise divine system for the reckoning of time.

The Septuagint translated the emphatic Hebrew *moth tamuth*, "you shall surely die" (Genesis 2:17 NKJV) with overly literal Greek, *thanatō apothaneisthe*, "dying you shall die." That suggested to Athanasius that the penalty for humanity's departure from its proper path was "not dying merely, but abiding ever in the corruption of death." Without sin the first humans would have experienced death as a physical process but not corruption and separation from God.[93]

(The point here is not that the Septuagint rendering is correct but that a prominent church father apparently understood humanity's original condition to include biological mortality.)

Luther agreed with the general Western tradition that if humans had not sinned they would not have died. He speculated that eventually a sinless Adam would have fallen into sleep like that which God brought upon him to form Eve and "would have been changed and transported into the spiritual life without experiencing any pain."[94] We might ask, could this not also be seen as a description of a blessed death?

Of course none of this should be taken to mean that any Christian theologian before the nineteenth century understood the actual situation of the earliest humans, who would have been subject to diseases, accidents, predation, the processes of aging and other expressions of mortality. But the idea that the physical death of humans is a consequence of sin is not as firmly established in the Christian tradition as is sometimes thought.

After the man and woman eat of the forbidden tree, God expels them from the garden because the human "might reach out his hand and take also from the tree of life, and eat, and live forever" (Genesis 3:22). What is in view here, as James Barr has argued,[95] is not the loss of a freedom from death that humanity once possessed but the loss of an *opportunity* for immortality. Humanity is pictured here as "dust" animated by the breath, or spirit, of God, and without God's ongoing sustenance will return to dust (Genesis 2:7 and 3:19, Psalm 104:29).

We do, however, need to take seriously Paul's statements that "sin came into the world through one man, and death came through sin" (Romans 5:12) and that "all die in Adam" (1 Corinthians 15:22). In order to deal with these challenges, in the following chapter we will consider both the limited scientific understanding of the biblical writers and the fact that death involves more than a stoppage of biological machinery.

Transmitting Humanness

The phrase "human nature" has been avoided up to this point because it can convey the idea that there is some fixed essence of humanness. In fact, that is exactly the meaning of the phrase in the philosophies of Hellenistic origin that for a long time played a major role in Christian theology. But that idea does not fit well with the dynamic picture of the world, and of biological systems in particular, in modern science. Change is relatively slow but it does take place. The things that make us distinctively human, our biology and our culture, are also the things that pass on our humanity, with small changes (Darwin's "descent with modification"[96]) to those who come after us.

It is our genetic endowment that makes us members of our particular biological species. This particular genotype was formed by many millions of years of evolution, with environmental factors and competition between members of our ancestral types winnowing out genetic combinations that were less favorable for survival. The mention of competition should not be taken to mean that biological evolution involves only bloody warfare, "nature red in tooth and claw." There are also cooperative aspects of the evolutionary process.[97] But natural selection means that competition does play a crucial role, and the old saying that "All's fair in love and war" applies to it. We can surmise that the earliest humans possessed tendencies for violence, deception, theft, and sexual promiscuity, and that is to some extent confirmed by observations of our closest surviving primate relatives.[98]

But these are only capabilities. Genes do not produce results quite as inexorably as many popular presentations suggest. Even for purely biological phenomena they often result only in *tendencies*. A woman who has a "gene for breast cancer" will, all other things being equal, be more likely to develop a malignancy than will one without that gene but in neither case will the gene, or a lack thereof, lead by itself with certainty to one result or another. And with far more complex behavioral phenomena there is no evidence that particular genes or sets of them will always lead to determined patterns of activity. The defense "My genes made me do it" can always be rejected, though some consideration can be given to "My genes encouraged me to do it."

We are not just reducible to our genes—or to put it another way, we are not purely biological entities. From the time when our ancestors starting communicating with one another, using crude tools and passing on information to offspring, we have been characterized by another feature—culture. Humans are, as Philip Hefner has put it, a "symbiosis" of biology and culture.[99] Neither "nature" alone nor "nurture" alone provides an adequate description of what it means to be human.

Culture like biology changes, and the term "cultural evolution" is often used to parallel our understanding of biological change. This language can be misleading, however, since people often take it to mean that the development of culture can be subsumed under a general heading of "evolution" understood in "Darwinian" terms – that is, by natural selection. While selection does play a role in cultural change, it is by no means the only, or even the most important, factor. Education, formal or not, is an essential element in the transfer of culture from one generation to another, and this is a process of "transmission of acquired characters." That was how Lamarck, before Darwin and Wallace, tried to explain biological evolution, and in that realm it doesn't work.[100] The so-called "central dogma" of genetics is that information passes from germ cells to bodies, not *vice versa*. One classic illustration is the fact that a blacksmith will not pass on to his children the powerful arm muscles that he has developed in the course of his work. But the blacksmith can (and in a traditional culture probably will) teach his sons how to work in a smithy. If we may oversimplify considerably, biology is Darwinian and culture is Lamarckian.

Both biology and culture can play roles in inculcating altruistic behavior toward one's kinship group. By helping close relatives to survive and have offspring, you will help to pass on genes that you share with that person. Of course, most cultures tell people that they should favor and care for members of their family or tribe. Why people should behave in that way toward humans with whom there is no obvious relationship, let alone toward members of other species is (in spite of the efforts of some sociobiologists) a biological mystery. "Altruism toward strangers," as Mayr says, "is a behavior not supported by natural selection."[101] The fact that such trans-kin altruism does take place, that people are helpful to strangers, sometimes at considerable expense, and expend time and energy to protect the habitats of birds or rescue stray cats, is a cultural phenomena.

We cannot simply leave it at that however, because trans-kin altruism is, from a Christian standpoint, a crucial aspect of humanity. We are called to love even our enemies (Matthew 5:43-48) and to represent the God of whom it is said, "The compassion of human beings is for their neighbors, but the compassion of the Lord is for every living thing" (Sirach 18:13). As Hefner again puts it: "Trans-kin altruism is not merely a scientifically puzzling phenomenon, nor a regrettably neglected virtue; it is a central symbol and ritual of what human beings should be doing with their lives."[102]

But obviously humanity is capable of other kinds of behavior as well. Racism and wars of aggression are cultural phenomenon, as are hunting for sport and the staging of cock fights. Science by itself cannot tell us which kinds of culturally encouraged behavior are good and which are evil. Humans engage in murder, rape, torture, pillage, and environmental devastation, and in fact do so far beyond any degree that could be plausibly explained by natural selection. Human history often seems to be, in Gibbon's words, "little more than the register of the crimes, follies, and misfortunes of mankind."[103] We can analyze this unpleasant reality from a number of different standpoints, but theologically it means that something has gone wrong with God's creation.

Homo Religiosus

Paul began his address to the Athenians on Mars Hill by noting that he had observed how "extremely religious" they were (Acts 17:22). Athens was hardly unique, for religion has long been a pervasive feature of most cultures. Burial practices and cave art show that some of the earliest humans (*Homo sapiens* and perhaps Neanderthals as well) had "religion"—that is, practices, beliefs, and ideas that we recognize today as religious.[104]

Questions about how and why religion arose and why it persists are of interest from both scientific and theological standpoints. One rather common idea has been that religion provided an explanation for natural phenomena that we now understand scientifically: People used to understand diseases as divine punishments or the depredations of evil demons, but we now know about bacteria and viruses. But while people certainly used to think of diseases in that way, this fails to explain why cultures continue to be religious even when people know about scientific medicine. There have, of course, been other attempts to explain away religion, like psychological theories popular in the heyday of Freudianism.

More recently there have been attempts to elucidate the persistence of religion in terms of genetics and/or features of the brain.[105] Biological anthropologist Barbara King does not discount these factors but, from the standpoint of one who studies primate behavior, focuses on the need for connection and belonging that can already be observed in monkeys and apes. The "bottom line," she concludes, is that "hominids turned to the sacred realm because they evolved to relate in deeply emotional ways with their social partners, because the resulting mutuality engendered its own creativity and generated increasingly nuanced expressions of belongingness over time, and because the human brain evolved to allow an extension of this belongingness beyond the here and now."[106]

All these ideas can be encompassed within a theological understanding of the human. God acts through created things, and that may include God's use of aspects of our genomes and brains and features that have developed within our cultures in order to make people aware of the divine presence. But there are two distinctively theological points that need to be borne in mind.

God initiates communication with creatures, not the other way around. In the biblical story God or a messenger from God speaks with Adam, Abraham, Moses, Mary, and others. There may be some degree of preparation or readiness for such communication on the part of people, but even that has to be seen as something that has developed ultimately because of the way in which God has acted previously, and perhaps without human awareness, in the lives of those people. That divine initiative is clear when God tells Jeremiah that "Before I formed you in the womb I knew you, and before you were born I consecrated you" (Jeremiah 1:5). "Our hearts are restless till they find rest in thee," Augustine said, but that is because "thou hast formed us for thyself."[107]

Secondly, the fact that people are religious does not necessarily mean that they have genuine faith in the true God. Emotional connections, belonging to a group, or understanding the patterns of our world and our own existence are things that *we* need and want, and we can seek them for our own benefit. Barth distinguished between "religion" as a human attempt to justify oneself before God (or whatever ultimate court one thinks there is) and God's revelation that contradicts human presuppositions. Bonhoeffer wrote that "the Christian is not a *homo religiosus*, but simply a man, as Jesus was a man."[108]

Religious behaviors can be expressions of evil. Human sacrifice in the cultures of Mesoamerica, the burning of heretics by Christians and the terrorist attacks of September 11, 2001 by Muslims are obvious examples. There have also been and still are other religious practices that are not as bloody but are still oppressive. Evidence for religious practices of early humans should not automatically be taken as indications of positive spiritual development. They may instead be signs that humans had refused to accept God's initial offers of fellowship and were trying, in confused ways of their own devising, to take hold of what God wanted to give them.

As we have considered our views of death, the ways in which we behave, and our propensities for religion, we have continued to come up against the idea that something has gone wrong with creation. Things are not as God intended for them to be. That "going wrong," the threat to creation posed by sin, will be addressed in the next chapter.

CHAPTER IV

CREATION UNDER THREAT

The Human Problem

The use of any of the terms traditionally applied to the work of Christ—salvation, reconciliation, atonement, redemption, and others —implies that something is wrong with humanity and perhaps with the wider creation as well, and that this defect is to be remedied. In order to talk about salvation we must first ask what we need to be saved from. In order to talk about redemption, we need at ask what we're to be "bought back" from. And in order to talk about atone-ment or reconciliation, we must ask what has kept us and God apart. The basic answer to all those questions is "sin," and the Bible has several ways of speaking about this.

1 John 3:4 puts it very simply: "Sin is lawlessness." This seems to be just the popular understanding of sin—breaking God's rules. It is important to realize, though, that the law in question is not a set of arbitrary regulations, "conditions for membership of some fantastic club like the Red-Headed League."[109] The most important command-ments which in themselves summarize the law (Mark 12:29-31 and parallels)—love of God with one's whole being above all else and love for neighbor as oneself—are statements about what is necessary if humans are to be in the right relationship with their creator and with the rest of creation. "Lawlessness" then is anything opposed to, or outside of, the patterns which God intends for creation.

The second table of the law is about relations among humans. We are to respect authority, the lives and property of others, marriage, and truth. Even before these laws are formalized at Sinai, the com-missions given to humanity in the creation stories establish broader responsibilities. The human calling is to "have dominion" over the earth in a way that represents God's love and care for the world (Gen-esis 1:26-28). We are, as Genesis 2:15 tells us, to "serve" and "guard" the garden. In accord with these verses, Torah has a number of regulations—most notably those for the Sabbath of the land and the year of Jubilee (Leviticus 25)—for the care of the earth and its creatures together with justice among humans.[110] The reality of sin is that we don't do a very good job with any of those things. Whether "traditional" sins such as murder, theft, and adultery, or the destruction of the natural environment which has only recently come to be recognized as sinful, sin has been a pervasive feature of human history since its beginnings.

The fundamental sin is against the first commandment. Nothing is to come ahead of the true God. The first commandment is not about an abstract monotheism, for it is "the LORD your God, who brought you out of the land of Egypt, out of the house of slavery" (Exodus 20:1) who is to come first. We are, as Luther explains this, to "Fear, love, and trust God above all things." All the other commandments really depend on this one, as Luther makes clear by beginning the explanation of each of them with the words "We are to fear and love God, so that . . ."[111] And again, of course, we all put many things ahead of the true God, including perhaps some that we may imagine *are* God.

Paul gives this sin a significant emphasis in Romans 1. It is the refusal to acknowledge the true God *as creator*, the insistence instead on making idols, which is the fundamental human problem (Romans 1:18-23). Those idols are usually more subtle than the "images resembling a mortal human being or birds or four-footed animals or reptiles" that Paul refers to in verse 23. "Mortal," God said to Ezekiel when some of the elders came to consult him, "these men have taken their idols into their hearts" (Ezekiel 14:3). Our fundamental problem is putting our trust in creatures (sometimes creatures of our imagination, sometimes ourselves) instead of the creator. That is Sin with a capital S, and all the other sins which Paul then lists in verses 26-31—sexual immorality, murder, slander, deceit, etc.—are consequences of it. Sin is rejection of the creator, and this inevitably results in disruption of creation.

There are two biblical words for sin that are of special interest for our later discussion. The Hebrew *chata'* has the sense of erring or missing a target. (That literal meaning occurs in Judges 20:16.) In the New Testament, the Greek verb commonly used for sin, *hamartia*, also meant originally to miss the mark.[112] Both words have the basic sense of failing to achieve an intended goal. While they do not have connotations of moral culpability as strong as some other terms, they suggest a significant concept: going in the wrong direction. If creation is dynamic, if God created the world with the intention that it move toward the goal described in Ephesians 1:10, then it is a serious problem if creation, or part of it, is moving in such a way as to fail to reach that goal.

The same idea can be discerned in the most common word for "repent" in the Old Testament, *shubh*, which means to turn back or return. If you are going away from where you are supposed to end up, you can get to your goal only by changing course. Thus in a classic text calling for repentance from the book of Joel (2:12-17), one that is often read on Ash Wednesday, God says, "Return to me with all your heart," and the prophet repeats, "Return to the LORD your God, for he is gracious and merciful, slow to anger and abounding in steadfast love."

This image of taking the wrong path and moving away from God is a way of picturing what has happened to humanity as a whole. And if humanity is given the responsibility to care for creation that is sketched in Genesis 1:26-28 and 2:15, the fact that we have gotten off course will have serious consequences for the rest of earth's creatures as well. The environmental problems of which we finally began to be aware in the second half of the twentieth century are prominent signs of this. As a consequence of human sin Jeremiah (4:23) saw the earth "waste and void" and heavens that "had no light." Those phrases suggest a reversal of the first creation story of Genesis. New creation is not just God putting the final touches on the original work of creation, it is also God pulling creation away from a course that leads to destruction.

Sins of Men and Women

The fundamental sin, then, is failure to put one's trust, first and foremost, in the true God. This means a failure to acknowledge God as the creator of one's life, a failure that then disrupts relationships among creatures. Thus sin threatens God's creation, and that can be expressed in more than one way.

The clearest expression of sin has been seen traditionally as pride, *superbia*, which can reach even the extreme of the creature putting self in the place of God. The biblical story of human sin begins with a seductive offer in the Garden of Eden: "You will be like God, knowing good and evil" (Genesis 3:5). The prophets often denounce the pride of rulers of Israel and the nations. The sin of the prince of Tyre which will bring the Deep over him and his wealthy city is that "your heart is proud and you have said, 'I am a god; I sit in the seat of the gods, in the heart of the seas,' yet you are a mortal and no god, though you compare your mind with the mind of a god" (Ezekiel 28:2). A similar message is conveyed by the "broken myth" of Isaiah 14:12-21. Here the story of how the younger Canaanite gods fell when they tried to storm the mount of the elder gods to take their place is used as a taunt song over the king of Babylon.[113]

A great deal of the sin which has afflicted the human race can indeed be traced to pride of this sort. There have been relatively few men who have claimed to be, literally, God or a god, but more who have imagined themselves to be God's unique representative, and many who simply think and act without regard for any authority higher than themselves. Atheists can do the same thing without the use of "God" language. "We must be ruthless," said the Bolshevik Bukharin, "Because the *sword of history* is in our hand."[114] Political and economic oppression, wars of aggression, slavery and maintenance of other oppressive social structures, and rape as an expression of power are all ways in which pride bears fruit. Its effects are not limited to the human sphere, for man's self-serving exploitation of the earth has caused a great deal of environmental damage and destruction of other species. Reinhold Niebuhr is just one theologian who saw the basic sin as pride, the fact that man "always usurps God's place and claims to be the final judge of human actions."[115]

But there is a reason why in the last two paragraphs I abandoned gender inclusive language and used masculine terms in speaking of this desire to usurp the place of the creator. When the voices of women began to be heard in theological discussions some fifty years ago, challenging questions were raised about the idea of pride as a universal model for sin.

First, women have often been the chief victims of this sin of pride. It has generally been males who have aspired to "be as gods," and religious, social and economic structures which legitimize the belief that men naturally are to rule women have had an abusive effect. Many criticisms of the treatment of women in cultures influenced by Christianity have focused on ways in which they are oppressed as a result of masculine pride. That does not, in itself, invalidate the belief that pride is the root sin. It simply points out that the Christian tradition has, until recently, failed to see that women most often have been victims of this sin. If anything it has helped to bring out the serious consequences of pretenses to divinity.

The feminist analysis, however, goes deeper than this. Women, already subjugated by exercises of masculine pride, had been told that they should not have "proud" aspirations to fulfill their lives beyond the bounds set for them by patriarchal authority. Rebellion against that authority is seen as a repetition of the sin of Eve, whose desire to be like God was, according to patriarchal analysis, responsible for the troubles of the human race. Good women should know their place, under the authority of men.

That traditional analysis fails to see, or does not want to see, that there is another type of sin. We can want to be more than what we should be, but we can also be content to be less than what we should be. This was pointed out in 1960 in an influential article by Valerie Saiving, who argued that while men may be prone to sins characterized by "pride" and "will to power," women tend to sins that can be summarized as "underdevelopment or negation of the self."[116] Since then a number of other feminist theologians have expanded upon this insight.[117] Women are tempted not to rule the world but to ignore God's call to make full use of the abilities they have been given and to exercise responsible dominion. It has been easy for them to accommodate themselves to patriarchal structures and to let someone else make the decisions and exercise power.

Does the difference in propensity to these types of sins have some biological basis or is a purely cultural phenomenon?[118] Do men want to rule and are women content to be ruled because of X and Y chromosomes or simply because both women and men were for many generations accustomed to those patterns? The latter option is suggested by the fact that large parts of Western and other societies, as well as many Christian churches, have gradually dropped restrictions on the leadership roles which women may play, and are, with some struggle, adjusting to gender equality.

It would be too simplistic to suggest that all males are beset by overweening pride or that no females try to take control of the situations in which they live. The reality of different types of sin has been recognized independently of their correlations with gender. We might think of the man who buried his master's money in Jesus' parable (Matthew 25:14-30) as an illustration of the sin of failing to use our gifts, and the general confessions used in church services often include recognition of both the wrong things that have been done and the right ones that have *not* been done. Barth distinguished three "forms" of sin, pride, sloth, and falsehood.[119] Calling one type of sin "masculine" and another "feminine" is shorthand, with statistical accuracy at best. But because the distinction does have a good deal to do with ways in which women have been subordinated to men in many traditional cultures, the terminology remains helpful.

In any case we have identified two different ways in which human beings can resist God's will for creation—by trying to usurp the role of the creator and by refusing to be what God has called us to be in creation. We should not expect that either will be eliminated by merely human effort, and in fact may see the progress that has been made toward equality of opportunity for women and men as part of the working out of the atoning work of Christ which we will be discussing later. The fundamental point here is that both types of sin are distortions of creation.

The Universality of Sin

The fact that humanity has come into being through the processes of evolution causes no major problems for the doctrine of creation. We noted in Chapter II that this can be understood as an example of God's activity in the world through natural processes. But when we come to the topics of sin and salvation, opponents of both evolution and Christianity, strange bedfellows though they are, quickly agree in pointing to what they see as a devastating contradiction. Christianity, it is claimed, absolutely requires that the story of "the Fall" in Genesis 3 be a true historical narrative. "If there was no historical Adam and no historical Fall, the need for a savior disappears," the argument goes. "The structure of Christianity collapses." We already noted such a claim made by John Spong in our first chapter, but it is worth emphasizing the extent to which this idea is responsible for creating the impression that Christianity and evolution are fundamentally incompatible.[120]

Evolution does require that we rethink traditional ideas about righteousness, sin, and salvation. But the basic Christian claim is that a savior is needed because all people are sinners. It is that simple: "Since all have sinned and fall short of the glory of God, they are now justified by his grace as a gift, through the redemption that is in Christ Jesus" (Romans 3:23-24). *Why* all people are sinners is an important question which we need to investigate (for it will influence our understanding of *how* Christ saves us), but an answer is not required in order to recognize the need for salvation. None of the gospels uses the story in Genesis 3 to speak of the significance of the work of Christ. In Romans Paul develops an indictment of the human race as sinful and then presents Christ as God's solution to this problem in chapters 1-3 before speaking about Adam's sin in chapter 5. It is the fact that all human beings are sinners, rather than a theory about how that condition arose, that requires a savior.

In support of this claim we can cite Jonathan Edwards. Writing in the eighteenth century, he was unaware of modern evolutionary theories and read Genesis 3 as history. Yet the first chapter of his defense of the doctrine of original sin is "The Evidence of Original Sin from What Appears in Fact of the Sinfulness of Mankind."[121] In proclaiming the Christian message to people who haven't heard it, we don't begin by trying to convince them that there was a sin of the first humans in which they were involved. The basic law-gospel message is simply "you are a sinner and Christ is your savior."

It is important to emphasize that the evidence to which Edwards appealed was that of scripture, not humanity's common experience that people act badly. It is sometimes said that original sin is the most empirically obvious Christian doctrine, but this is misleading. Sin has to do first of all with our relationship with God. It is obvious that all people think and do bad things at times, but only revelation tells us that everyone is alienated from God and acts contrary to God's will. "Through the law comes the knowledge of sin" (Romans 3:20).

The crucial distinction that needs to be made here is between the idea of a sin which took place at the beginning of human history (*peccatum originale originans*, "original sin as originating") and that of a sin which affects all human beings from the beginning of their lives and from which they cannot free themselves (*peccatum originale originatum*, "original sin as originated").[122] The need for a savior depends on the latter belief but not the former. The term "original sin" is often used for both concepts, sometimes interchangeably with "sin of origin." For the sake of clarity, and to avoid the use of Latin terms or clumsy translations, I will, in what follows, use "original sin" for the idea of a first sin of humankind while "sin of origin" will refer to the idea that each human begins life in a sinful condition.

Sin is an existential reality: Each of us is a sinner and we share a common sinful condition. Many modern theologians have tried to keep this point in view without reading Genesis 3 as history,[123] and some are explicit about getting rid of Adam and Eve as historical figures.[124] Genesis 2—3 should not be read as historical in anything like the modern sense of an account of events "as they really happened." Adam and Eve are to be seen as theological representations of all humans, and we need not try to locate the first parents of the human race in the paleontological record.

A discussion of atonement necessitated by the empirical reality of the universal character of human sin alone would be severed from a broader understanding of the world to which both the doctrine of creation and our scientific knowledge point. The historical origin of sin is not the article by which the church stands or falls, but it demands consideration if we want the message we proclaim to make sense to people.

If Adam and Eve represent *all* humans then they represent also the *first* humans. And if humanity has been sinful from the time that it came into being, without doing anything to *become* sinful, sin would be part of the original human condition. This would mean that in an important sense God is the creator of sin. To avoid this conclusion we must try to understand how the earliest human sin might have had a role in bringing about a sinful condition as part of the evolutionary process.

Genesis 3 is about humans distrusting and disobeying God: They don't believe what God has said and transgress God's command. The story is not, first of all, about sins of one human against another. This sin against God does, however, result in fractured relationships of people with one another and with the world. The man blames the woman, who blames the serpent. Sin casts a shadow on childbearing and a curse (which we will consider later) on the ground. In the following chapters the situation worsens with Cain's murder of Abel, Lamech's cry for unlimited vengeance, the universal corruption of humanity that provokes the flood, and the story of the Tower of Babel with the resultant disruption of human community. What is pictured is not so much a single abrupt "fall" in Genesis 3 as it is a process of falling throughout chapters 3-11. (It is interesting that some early Jewish and Christian writers—for example, the Book of Jubilees and Irenaeus—thought that Cain's sin was worse than Adam's.[125])

But what of the idea that this first sin is passed on, or imputed, to all descendants of Adam? The early chapters of Genesis and, indeed, the whole Old Testament say nothing of that. There is no indication that the writer of Genesis 3 thought of the sin of Adam and Eve as a causal factor in the general sinfulness of humanity. A general sinfulness is, however, in view. In Genesis 8:21, after the rest of humanity has been destroyed and only Noah's family remains, God observes that "the inclination of the human heart is evil from youth." Psalm 51:5 and Job 14:1-4 suggest that this general sinfulness affects every person from the beginning of life.

By the time of Christ, however, Jews were understanding Adam and Eve as historical figures and their sin as the cause of later human misery. Paul's statements about Adam are to be read in that context. But care is needed against excesses of both "conservative" and "liberal" interpretation.

On one hand, the fact that Judaism of the time, and Paul himself, thought of Adam as an historical figure doesn't mean that we must understand Adam in that way. I argued in Chapter II that the divine *kenosis* should be considered in connection with the inspiration of scripture, and that outdated information about the physical world in Genesis should be seen as a result of the Holy Spirit accommodating inspiration to the state of human knowledge in the cultures of the biblical writers. That was not just a matter of authors using elementary language to describe things that their contemporaries didn't understand. There is no reason to think that the writer of Genesis 1 knew about the big bang but chose to speak in terms of ancient near-eastern cosmology. We can understand Paul's references to Adam as an historical individual as similar accommodation by the Holy Spirit. Paul's purpose in Romans 5:12-21 was to state the importance of Christ for the human problems of sin and death, not to give information about the early history of humanity.[126]

On the other hand, saying that Adam was not an historical individual does not mean that Paul's discussion has no theological significance. He speaks in verse 12 of sin coming into the world, not as something simply given in creation. The spread of death is due to the fact that "all have sinned." Yet there is some difference between the sin of "all" and the primordial sin, for Paul refers (verse 14) to "those whose sins were not like the transgression of Adam." The first sin had some kind of causal efficacy: "By the one man's disobedience the many were made sinners" (5:19).

Paul does not say *how* one man's disobedience made many sinners. He does not refer to Adam as one "in whom all sinned," as the Latin translation of verse 12 which Augustine read (*in quo omnes peccaverunt*) puts it. Nor is there the idea of a forensic imputation of Adam's sin to all other humans, in supposed parallel to justification as forensic imputation of Christ's righteousness.[127] But Paul apparently did see more in Genesis 3 than the author of that text intended, and it would be wrong even on the level of secular literature to say that he was wrong to do so. We don't say that Goethe "misunderstood" the Faust story because he changed its meaning from earlier versions. And if we take the idea of inspiration of scripture seriously, it is not hard to believe that Paul could have been led to a deeper understanding than that of the earlier biblical author.

Ephesians 2:1-3 should also be noted here. This says nothing about an original sin of the first human beings, but the statement that before coming to faith people are "dead through the trespasses and sins in which you once lived" and "by nature children of wrath" affirms what we are calling sin of origin. The idea that all people are "children of God" is often expressed in liberal religion and there is a broad sense in which it is true (e.g., Acts 17:28), but this contrasts with the way in which Ephesians and also 1 John describe the human condition.

Sin of origin and original sin did not become contentious topics among Christians until the fifth century.[128] The issue came to a head in debates between Augustine of Hippo and the British monk Pelagius and their supporters.[129] Their disagreement was not first about the sin of Adam but over the extent to which human beings could do God's will without the special grace that is available because of the work of Christ.

Pelagius held that while it is God who makes it possible for people to will and do good works and even to remain sinless, people really can do those things. Sin is something we do, not something we are born with. In contrast, Augustine insisted that all people are sinful from the beginning of life. One of his arguments was that the church baptized infants, like adults, "for the forgiveness of sins" (in the words of the Nicene Creed), which would make no sense if infants were not in some sense sinners. Pelagius had a more optimistic view of unaided human powers. Augustine explained the sinfulness of all people as something transmitted from parents to children, and ultimately from Adam and Eve, because of the lust that is inevitably involved in sexual intercourse by sinful people.[130] For Pelagius, on the other hand, Adam essentially set a bad example that we *may* follow but don't *have to* follow.

The Western church generally accepted the views of Augustine. The definitive statement of this is the canons of the Synod of Orange in A.D. 529.[131] What is meant by "the doctrine of original sin" in Western Christianity is usually some version of Augustine's teaching: All people except Jesus receive the consequences of Adam's sin and are born not only with a tendency to sin but actually as sinners.[132] Different parts of the Christian tradition have, however, modified this view in various ways, and some Christians from Augustine's time to today have opposed his teaching. The idea that all people are "born sinful" is unpleasant, and especially since the Enlightenment many people have held a more positive view of the human condition. (The African slave trade, the Holocaust, and other great evils suggest some caution here, but hope springs eternal.) They have rejected the idea of a sin of origin, and while they may appeal to evolution to support their position, their basic reason for opposing the doctrine may in fact be their optimistic view of the human condition.

The ninth of the Articles of Religion of the Church of England, "Of Original or Birth-Sin," is a clear example of the Augustinian tradition:

> Original sin standeth not in the following of Adam (as the Pelagians do vainly talk); but it is the fault and corruption of the Nature of every man, that naturally is engendered of the offspring of Adam; whereby man is very far gone from original righteousness, and is of his own nature inclined to evil, so that the flesh lusteth always contrary to the Spirit; and therefore in every person born into this world, it deserveth God's wrath and damnation.[133]

This is a grim picture of the human condition, but even though it speaks of our nature as being corrupt and inclined to evil it does not simply identify sin of origin with human nature. That would mean that fallen humanity would no longer be God's creation, and thus be tantamount to the Manichean heresy which accords genuine creative power to evil. The Lutheran Formula of Concord, while taking a strong stand against Pelagianism, also explicitly rejected this opposite extreme.[134] Sinful human beings are still creatures of God and in essence good.

A discussion of the sin of origin would be incomplete if we did not ask: If sin is a defect or distortion, what is it a defect in or a distortion of?

The counterpart of "original sin" in classical theology is "original righteousness," the idea that humanity was created *without* sin and able to avoid it. Abraham Calovius defined the original condition of humanity according to this view.[135]

> It is called a state of integrity, because man in it was upright and uncorrupt (Ecclesiastes 7:29) in intellect, will, the corporeal affections and endowments, and in all things was perfect. They call it also the state of *innocence*, because he was innocent and holy, free from sin and pollution.

In this state humanity had true faith in the true God. As Calovius' statement shows, the idea was often elaborated in such a way that Adam and Eve were pictured as perfect in all respects, with physical and mental abilities far beyond those of later people, in addition to complete trust in their creator.

Speculations like that have exacerbated the apparent conflict between Christianity and evolution. In fact it is this idea of original righteousness, rather than doctrines of original sin or sin of origin, that are challenged most severely by the realities of evolution. This is unfortunate and unnecessary because, as we saw in the previous chapter, the Bible says nothing about any primordial perfection.[136] Genesis 1—3 does not say that the first humans were intellectually brilliant or had amazing physical powers. Even their ability to trust in God doesn't mean that they were skilled theologians.

In the traditions of the Eastern Church we find a picture of early humanity rather different from that of the West, and more in line with a developmental picture.[137] The second century apologist Theophilus of Antioch explained the prohibition of the tree of knowledge by saying, "Adam, being yet an infant in age, was on this account as yet unable to receive knowledge worthily."[138] According to Irenaeus, "The man was a young child, not yet having reached a perfect deliberation" and "It was necessary for him to reach full-development by growing in this way."[139] While for Augustine and the Western church the perfection of humanity was actually realized in Eden before the entry of sin, Irenaeus and much of the Eastern tradition think of humanity as created with potential to grow toward perfection. God gave humanity the ability to progress, with divine grace, toward full union with God. One result of this difference between Eastern and Western pictures of the original condition and sin of humanity is that "Orthodoxy, holding as it does a less exalted idea of man's state before he fell, is also less severe than the west in its view of the consequences of the fall." [140]

The views of the Eastern Church about the original state of humanity are more open to an evolutionary understanding than are traditional ideas in the West. (This is not to say that Orthodox Christians generally would deny that Adam and Eve were historical persons.) But we cannot simply take over without modification the Eastern picture of the sinful condition of humanity. There are ways in which the grimmer account of the human condition given by the Augustinian tradition seems more realistic. While the story of an abrupt fall from perfection is without biblical support, a picture of subsequent spiritual incapacity is warranted by scriptural texts like the image of spiritual death in Ephesians 2:1-5 and Paul's catena of quotations from the Psalms and Isaiah in Romans 3:10-18 to the effect that "There is no one who is righteous, not even one."

Evolution and Sin

The first humans in a theological sense were hominids in whom reason, self-awareness, and communication had developed to an extent that it was somehow possible for them to be aware of God's address to them. They could have understood God's will for them at least dimly. From this point on the term "human" will be used to refer to hominids with those qualities. They came into being through an evolutionary process in which natural selection was at least a major factor. The ancestors of those first humans would have been members of their species who were most successful in competition with others for food, breeding opportunities, protection from predators, and other survival needs.

Evolution would thus have endowed our prehuman ancestors with strong tendencies for selfish behavior.[141] While these behaviors would have had a strong biological component, culture - learning from other members of the species and especially the kinship group - would also have contributed to them. The biological component itself tends to propagate genes that are shared with close kin. But with that understood, our ancestors would have been driven to win out over others, by fair means or foul.

That latter phrase does not really apply to creatures who are not moral agents with knowledge of "fair" and "foul." Our prehuman ancestors cannot be called "immoral," let alone "sinful," because they killed, deceived, were sexually promiscuous, and did other things that would be sinful for their human descendants. But when the first humans, as we have defined them, came into being, they would have had strong propensities for the same types of behavior. When they began to become aware that such actions were contrary to God's will, these creatures would have been not just "moral agents" but, to coin a phrase, "theological agents." They would have been responsible to God for their actions, and some of the things they had done in the past would now be sinful.

But their inherited tendencies would have made it difficult for them to avoid acting in such ways. In other words, it would have been hard for them to obey what they knew of God's will for them. These implications of natural selection are theoretical, but we need not rely on theory alone. As we noted in the previous chapter, studies of our primate relatives have found that they behaved in ways that were consistent with what natural selection leads us to expect. While there are many examples of cooperative behavior among other primates, natural selection presents a serious challenge to the idea that the first humans lived in a sinless state of integrity for any period of time. It is not hard to believe that creatures who evolved through natural selection could have sinned. It is harder to make sense of the idea that the first humans were created in a condition in which they had a real possibility of *not* sinning.

How could a sin committed by the first humans result in a situation in which all later humans are sinners from the beginning of their lives? That condition has sometimes been called "hereditary sin" but it need not be understood as "genetic" in the sense that it is coded for by DNA. We know of conditions which are "hereditary"—inherited from a parent—but not "genetic," such as fetal alcohol syndrome. That birth defect is "inherited" from the mother but is caused by conditions of the uterine environment resulting from the mother's consumption of alcohol rather than by the genetic contribution of parents.

Let us imagine the earliest hominids—we do not have to decide where or when they lived, how many there were, or if they were a single group—who had evolved to the point of self-awareness and linguistic ability. The evolutionary course by which this condition was reached was one in which God was at work through natural processes. These humans had developed abilities to reason and communicate and were able in some way to receive and at least faintly understand God's Word, to trust in that Word, and obey God's will for them. We don't know in what way that expression of God's will may have come to them or what may have corresponded to the prohibition of the tree of knowledge in Genesis. It might have concerned the way in which people should live together harmoniously, but about that we can only speculate.

These first humans were at the beginning of a road along which God wanted to lead them and their descendants to fully mature humanity and complete fellowship with God. In principle they could follow that road but it would not be easy. They had inherited traits that enabled their ancestors to survive and pass on their genes. And those traits, as we have seen, would predispose them to some extent toward selfish behavior and away from the kind of community—with God, one another, and all creation—which God intended for them. Such behavior was not hardwired into them, but tendencies toward it were very strong. They could refuse to trust and disobey what they knew of God's will for them. In the language of Reinhold Niebuhr, sin was not "necessary" but it was "inevitable."[141]

History indicates this is what happened. We may consider first the evidence for religious ideas in burials, cave art, and perhaps even earlier artifacts. People sometimes see this as a positive feature of early humanity but, as we noted in the last chapter, religion is ambiguous. The basic human problem, as Paul describes it in Romans 1:18-31, is not that people are atheists but that they worship creatures rather than the creator. Primitive religious expressions may be a sign of estrangement from the true God. And it is all too obvious that the sexual immorality, violence, and dishonesty that Paul sees as consequences of refusal to honor the creator have marked humanity from its beginnings.

The biblical story indicates that this is an accurate *theological* description of what happened. The first humans took a wrong road, one "that leads to destruction" (Matthew 7:13), away from the goal that God intended. They and their descendants were soon alienated from God. Humanity was lost in the woods, darkness was falling, and the wolves were beginning to howl.

The previous paragraph is not an attempt to read the early chapters of Genesis as history. Purely secular history shows us that humanity has generally not known or worshipped the God of Israel and has been involved in conflict from its beginning. What the biblical story does is to provide a theological understanding of that history.

This image of "taking the wrong road," like that of "the fall," is a metaphor for the human condition, not an historical narrative. But the picture of gradual departure from the course God intended is, as we noted earlier, one which the early chapters of Genesis convey. It is important to emphasize that it is not the condition of being on a journey, of being in process, which is itself sinful. Being participants in the evolutionary process means being God's creatures, which is good. The problem of sin is not that we are on a road, but that we are on a *wrong* road.

The road metaphor is also not intended to mean that there was only one historical path that would lead to the goal God intended. Just as in our ordinary travels there may be a number of roads that will get us to our goal, as well as many that will take us far from it, so it would have been here.

Thus the model suggested here differs from those of process theology, for which Teilhard de Chardin is a good representative.[142] Teilhard comes close to calling sin a necessity, so that redemption is an aspect of creation: "One might even, perhaps, go so far as to say that since the creative act (by definition) causes being to rise up to God from the confines of nothingness . . . all creation brings with it, as its accompanying risk and shadow, some fault; in other words, it has its counterpart in some redemption."[143] I have argued, on the other hand, that while sin is "inevitable," it is not "necessary." Since the divine foreknowledge (and indeed just an understanding of what creation through the evolutionary process would produce) then envisioned sin, atonement was also foreseen.

So 1 Peter 1:19-20 and Revelation 13:8 can speak of Christ as the sacrificial lamb destined before or from (respectively) "the foundation of the world."[144] But redemption is not intrinsic to the very idea of creation.

Teilhard's picture is a straight line from God's initial creation through humanity's first sin and the cross-resurrection event to a final Omega point. In the model proposed here there are such theoretically possible histories but the real history of the world branched off when early humanity took the wrong road and started moving away from God's intended goal. God's redemptive activity, centering on the event of the cross, bends the course of history back toward God's goal.

In the Roman Catholic tradition original sin is understood to be the loss of a supernatural gift which God added to human nature, the *donum superadditum*. Lutheran and Reformed theologies, on the other hand, have understood it to be the loss of natural abilities, including the ability to have "true fear of God and true faith in God."[145] Because of this difference it is somewhat easier for the Roman tradition to deal with evolution because there the ability to have true faith was something added to the evolutionary process and the difficulties which we have suggested don't arise as strongly. This means, on the other hand, that the impact of original sin is to some extent reduced because humanity's natural endowments remain. The view suggested here sees original sin as being a matter of starting off in the wrong direction spiritually rather than losing something, original righteousness, which it once possessed.

We noted in the previous chapter that humans can be understood as a "symbiosis" of genes and culture. Both are good in the sense that they help to transmit to each person the essence of what we consider human. But both can also contribute to deviation from God's intention for humanity. Our genetic makeup, conditioned by natural selection, gives us powerful tendencies toward selfish behavior. The cultures in which we are conceived, born, and live exacerbate those tendencies in various ways. We are born as members of a tribe that is lost in the woods.

To say that there is a genetic component of original sin does not mean that there is a "gene for sin." Whether or not an action is sinful generally depends on the context in which it takes place as well as the action itself. And contrary to the "gene myth" which says that all our properties and behaviors are determined by DNA,[146] genes give us at most tendencies for certain behaviors.

To say that there is a cultural component of original sin means that sin is in part a result of our environment, an effect of "nurture" as well as "nature." This differs from the naïve view attributed to Pelagius, that Adam simply provides a bad example for us. The effects of our environment can be far more pervasive than that, as the analogy of fetal alcohol syndrome suggests. They are not things that we freely choose to accept or reject, but influences that we take in "with our mother's milk."

The universality of sin thus means more than that all people happen to sin. There is a solidarity in sin,[147] so that people make up a "lump of perdition" (*massa perditionis*) in the classic phrase. More modern language speaks of "structures of sin" such as racism and the culture of abortion in human societies. A person born in a racist society is not predestined to be a racist, but it will be very "natural" to become one. None of this, of course, means that individual sin is unimportant or can be blamed entirely on society. Our model does, however, increase the significance of this communal character of sin, giving it a causal role in the sin of origin.

The Greek noun *hamartia* can designate specific sinful acts, but in Paul and John it refers to "the sinful quality of life and the state of alienation from God."[148] A person who starts going in the wrong direction will have missed the mark even before he or she begins. Thus our sin of origin which points us in the wrong direction to start with truly is sin. As Tillich put it, "Before sin is an act, it is a state."[149]

Perhaps neither strict Augustinians nor determined Pelagians will be satisfied with this formulation. Unregenerate people are not compelled to sin, but all are sinners and would need God's help even if they could theoretically avoid "actual sins." The approach suggested here combines what seem to be the best insights of the Eastern and Western traditions. From the former we take a view of human origins and "first sin" that corresponds at least broadly with an evolutionary picture. With the latter we emphasize the reality and seriousness of each person's sin of origin. Thus we avoid both a picture of early humanity that contradicts scientific data and a view of human capabilities that clashes with the most searching insights into the law's demands and the human heart. The role of "cultural atmosphere" in keeping people from true faith in God does not mean that we have succumbed to Pelagianism. The fact that people *are* alienated from God and do not have such faith is a basic assumption, not something that we have first derived from our model and that has to be validated from it.

Having discussed the human problem (which is, at the same time, a problem for the wider creation), we can now begin to understand God's response. It will be a renewal of creation, not as a return to an imagined primordial state of perfection or as a total destruction of humanity and a creation of a new species, but a reorientation of creation to its proper goal. We begin discussion of this reconciliation in the next chapter.

Sin and Death

Both the writers and redactors of Genesis 2-3 as well as Paul in Romans and 1 Corinthians had in mind the physical death of humans when they spoke about "death" as a consequence of the sin of Adam and Eve. Two points must be made about that. The first is that just as the writers of Genesis were in error when they adopted the view of their culture that there was a dome of the heavens; biblical writers erred in adopting the views of their cultures that physical death of humans was a consequence of sin. As we saw earlier, the occurrence of these obsolete ideas in scripture should be understood as an aspect of divine *kenosis*.

Nevertheless, the early chapters of Genesis and the arguments that Paul developed from them tell us something of theological importance of death as an aspect of the human condition. When we speak of this we do have in mind physical death, the stopping of biological machinery. But this death also has powerful affects that we can hardly avoid. The sense of loss, the suffering that may be involved in dying, the uncertainty about what happens to the person who dies, revulsion at the idea of our bodies rotting, and the fact that we leave our work unfinished, may all be present. This is especially the case when we consider our own death or that of people we love, but it carries over even when we try to think about death quite objectively.

We can, however, consider the possibility that death wouldn't have had to be that way—that biological death might not have had all those affects. It might still have been puzzling and saddening, as it seems to be for the great apes, but not an object of horror and denial.[150] That could be the case if physical death were seen simply as a transition to some future life. And that is the way death *without* sin has sometimes been pictured in the Christian tradition. In the last chapter the remarks of Athanasius and Luther pointing in this direction were mentioned. We could also note C.S. Lewis' picture of the deaths of Martians in his science fiction novel, *Out of the Silent Planet*.[151]

The thing that makes death most terrible for those in the biblical tradition is that we are threatened with definitive separation from God. It is finally sin that makes death terrible, "the last enemy." Death has not only the affects mentioned before but also loss of God and fear of divine judgment. Those who live physically but without God can therefore be spoken of as "dead" (Ephesians 2:1-5), a condition of spiritual death.

When we look back over the history of life on earth from our standpoint as sinners (even if justified sinners) who have lived our whole lives in an atmosphere pervaded by sin, we see the dying that has taken place in evolutionary history, and especially the dying of human beings, as something more than merely physical death. It isn't really possible, especially for those who have been confronted and convicted by God's Word, to see human death as a purely biological phenomenon, separated from spiritual death.

In other words, sin gives new significance to death that has been occurring from the time that life on earth first developed. Human sin changes the *meaning* of physical death.[152] (This concept of what could be called "hermeneutical retrocausality" differs from the idea of transmission of physical signals back in time that may also find some theological applications.[153] But the attitude toward death of modern humans did not actually kill the dinosaurs!)

When Paul and other biblical writers spoke about death as a consequence of sin, they meant death as a totality—physical death with all the fears we have of it and in light of the separation from God that is sin. Death was a biological phenomenon plus spiritual death, though they did not make a neat separation of the two concepts. They were wrong about physical death being a consequence of human sin but right in seeing that it is sin that makes death an enemy that can be defeated only by God. Presumably the Holy Spirit was willing to accommodate inspiration to the incorrect aspects of their thought in order to allow the theologically important link between sin and spiritual death to be expressed.

CHAPTER V

RENEWING CREATION

The Renewal of Creation in the Bible

Creation and salvation are usually presented as two separate themes in theology. God created the world, something has gone wrong, and therefore creation (or part of it—some humans or perhaps only their souls) has to be saved. But the linkage is really much closer than that. God's supreme saving act in the Old Testament, the liberation of Israel from Egypt in the Exodus, can itself be seen as a work of creation, for Israel was in a real sense brought into being as a people in this event.[154] It is with good reason that from the earliest days of Christianity this has been seen as the supreme type of the passion and resurrection of Christ. In Luke's (9:28-36) account of the Transfiguration, Moses and Elijah are speaking with Jesus "of his departure [*exodon*], which he was about to accomplish at Jerusalem." The first verse of a classic Easter hymn by John of Damascus focuses entirely on the image of Israel's passage through the sea:

> Come, ye faithful, raise the strain of triumphant gladness!
> God hath brought his Israel into joy from sadness:
> Loosed from Pharaoh's bitter yoke
> Jacob's sons and daughters,
> Led them with unmoistened foot through the Red Sea waters.[155]

God's bringing of Israel through the sea also can be connected with creation by the use of the mythic motif of the *Chaoskampf*, God's battle with the sea and its monsters, called variously Rahab and Leviathan. Job 26:12-13, Psalm 74:12-17, Psalm 89:8-13, and Isaiah 51:9-10 belong in the category of what Brevard Childs has called "broken myth."[156] The biblical writers used pagan stories of primordial battles with the chaotic sea in which gods created the world to speak of the work of Israel's God.[157] In the last of those passages the mythic imagery is clear when God is pictured as the one "who cut Rahab in pieces" and "pierced the dragon." But the next two lines,

Renewing Creation • 71

"Was it not you who dried up the sea, the waters of the great deep; who made the depths of the sea a way for the redeemed to cross over?" obviously refer to the Exodus. The name Rahab can, significantly, be used for Egypt (cf. Psalm 87:4 and Isaiah 30:7).

Salvation can also be spoken of as divine renewal of creation in the Bible. The phrase "New heavens and new earth" is, with slight variations, found four times. Two of these are in the closing chapters of Isaiah, at 65:17 and 66:22-23. In the first of these God says, "For I am about to create [with the verb *br'*, expressing the divine prerogative of creation as in Genesis 1] new heavens and a new earth; the former things shall not be remembered or come to mind." This may suggest that there will be complete discontinuity between the present order of things and the new creation. But the second passage suggests some link between the two: "For as the new heavens and the new earth, which I will make, shall remain before me, says the LORD; so shall your descendants and your name remain. From new moon to new moon, and from sabbath to sabbath, all flesh shall come to worship before me, says the LORD."

In Revelation 21:1 the seer "saw a new heaven and a new earth; for the first heaven and the first earth had passed away, and the sea was no more." The elimination of the sea represents the end of the destructive forces which threaten creation. But what are we to make of the passing away of the present heaven and earth? Read in isolation, this would again suggest that the present order of things is simply to be annihilated in order to make way for the new. But later in the same chapter, when the new Jerusalem has come down from heaven, we are told that "the kings of the earth" (who up to this point in the book have been warring and oppressing God's people) "will bring their glory into it" (verse 24). The point is reiterated two verses later: "People will bring into it the glory and the honor of the nations" (verse 26). That glory and honor must be all the good that has been accomplished throughout the course of history.[158] There will be continuity in that what is good in the old creation will be preserved. All the good accomplished in world history enters into the holy city. But there is discontinuity in that "nothing unclean will enter it, nor anyone who practices abomination or falsehood" (verse 27). There is a similar emphasis in 2 Peter 3:13, which says that "We wait for new heavens and a new earth, where righteousness is at home."

Paul uses the explicit phrase "new creation" (*kainē ktisis)* twice, the only two occurrences of it in the Bible. A literal rendering of 2

Corinthians 5:17 is, "For if anyone is in Christ, a new creation." The relation between the indefinite "anyone" (*tis*) and the "new creation" is perhaps not obvious, and NRSV does not really explain it with "if anyone is in Christ, there is a new creation." Surely Paul does not mean that a renewal of the entire universe is dependent upon the status of any individual believer! The only reason not to accept the older translations typified by RSV and NIV—"if anyone is in Christ, he is a new creation"—is their non-inclusive language.[159] But that can easily be taken care of with the rendering "Anyone who is in Christ is a new creation."

The point is that the difference between old and the new is determined for people by their relationship with Christ. A person is a new creation by virtue of being "in Christ." This is not quite as obvious in Paul's second reference to new creation, Galatians 6:15, which states its absolute priority over both circumcision and uncircumcision. But when we read that in context and remember that the whole thrust of the letter to the Galatians is that Christ, rather than the regulations of Torah, is determinative of a person's relationship with God, we can see again that there is an equation of new creation with being in Christ. This is made especially clear in Galatians 3:28, where the transcendence of limitations of the old creation is a result of people being united "in Christ."

In both cases Paul refers "new creation" to the human sphere, but this does not mean that he (and the Bible generally) see only humanity as the object of reconciliation. Colossians 1:20, which speaks of the reconciliation of "all things" to God through the cross, and Romans 8:18-25, which looks forward to the liberation of "the creation" from bondage, make that clear. This must be emphasized over against commentators who try to limit the referents of these passages to humanity in spite of the fact that the language of these texts obviously has a wider scope.[160]

There are also texts that speak of personal renewal with other language. We might think first of the psalmist's prayer of repentance: "Create in me a clean heart, O God, and put a new and right spirit within me" (Psalm 51:10). Again the use of the verb *br'* is significant. The concept of being "born from above" or "born anew" in John 3:1-8 is also found in other texts which connect the new birth with baptism (Titus 3:5 and probably 1 Peter 1:3). The "born again" theme has, of course, been heavily emphasized in some parts of the Christian community, but not always with full awareness of its significance. Too often it seems to be identified simply with an individual decision or an emotional experience. The idea reaches its full expression when it is understood as a re-creative work of God rather than any choice by the one who is reborn. The very language of being brought to birth and the essentially passive role of one who becomes incorporated into the Christian community in Baptism point to new birth as a distinctive act of God.

In other texts God's saving work is connected or paralleled with the original creation of the world. The prologue of the Fourth Gospel begins by echoing the opening verse of the Bible with "In the beginning." That gospel text about the Word through whom "all things came into being" (John 1:3) reminds us of the important role that the creative power of the Word plays throughout the Bible. In the Johannine prologue it is connected with the concept of new creation through the statement that those who believe in the Word are given power to become children of God. And the re-creative power of the Word is displayed later in the Gospel when Jesus calls Lazarus forth from the tomb in fulfillment of John 5:25.

The Old Testament's image of God's victory over the sea is also picked up in the accounts of Jesus coming to the disciples on the sea (Mark 6:45-52 and parallels). These should be described not as Jesus walking on the water (in spite of the headings given to these sections in the UBS Greek text and the NRSV) but of him walking on the *sea* (Mark 6:48). To think of these stories simply as accounts of Jesus miraculously staying afloat misses their point. They (as well as the story of the stilling of the storm in Mark 4:35-41) mean that Jesus is the one who conquers the forces of chaos that threaten creation.

Renewal in the Christian Tradition

Themes related to new creation have been discussed, with greater or lesser emphases, throughout the course of Christian thought. We need not engage here in an exhaustive historical survey or analyze all the developments of the idea, but it will be helpful to note some references to it that are of particular interest for this discussion of atonement.

Modern theologians have made use of related concepts in different ways. We may note a brief discussion of Schillebeeckx in which Christology is spoken of as "intensified creation."[161] Tillich's emphasis on "new being" is also of interest here.[162] He speaks of this in terms of "*re*-conciliation, *re*-union, *re*-surrection." But the way in which

Tillich explicitly divorced the latter concept from future bodily resurrection means that his position is not adequate for a theology that takes the physical universe seriously.

Of course the word "new" does not have to be used in order to express the theme of new creation. A statement of Bonhoeffer's will set the stage for part of our discussion in the next chapter.[163]

> [T]he God of creation, of the utter beginning, is the God of the resurrection. The world exists from the beginning in the sign of the resurrection of Christ from the dead. Indeed it is because we know the resurrection that we know of God's creation in the beginning, of God's creating out of nothing. The dead Jesus Christ of Good Friday is the resurrected • • •• ••of Easter Sunday—that is creation out of nothing, creation from the beginning. The fact that Christ was dead did not provide the possibility of his resurrection but its impossibility; it was nothing itself, it was *nihil negativum*. There is absolutely no transition, no continuum between the dead Christ and the resurrected Christ, but the freedom of God that in the beginning created God's work out of nothing. Were it possible to intensify the *nihil negativum* even more, we would have to say here, in connection with the resurrection, that with the death of Christ on the cross the *nihil negativum* broke its way into God's own being: O great desolation! God, yes God, is dead. Yet the one who is the beginning lives, destroys the nothing, and in his resurrection creates the new creation. By his resurrection we know about the creation.

Anselm's model of atonement, in which Christ makes satisfaction to God for sin, is often presented with little if any reference to creation.[164] But Anselm himself saw an important connection. God's honor which had to be vindicated means that God's intention for creation had to be fulfilled. God had meant for a definite number of rational souls to enter the heavenly city and had created the angels for that purpose. However, part of the angels fell so that some of the intended number would have been lacking, and God created humanity to make up this lack. Since humanity also sinned, it was necessary for some to be saved so that the proper number of souls would be in the eschatological city.[165] God's purpose for creation would thus be fulfilled.

Anselm does not, however, connect the salvific work of Christ with his role as the agent of creation. The reason that the Son, rather than the Father or the Holy Spirit, became incarnate is explained with weak arguments, such as the claim that it is most appropriate for the Son to pray to the Father.

For our purposes, the greatest interest lies in the writings of earlier theologians in the Greek tradition. With Athanasius' Axiom in mind it is natural to look first to that theologian's early treatise. *On the Incarnation.* The basic human problem for Athanasius is that after humans had been created and given the chance for participation in the life of God, their choice of sin set them on the way back to non-being. "For transgression of the commandment was turning them back to their natural state, so that just as they have had their beginning out of nothing, so also, as might be expected, they might look for corruption into notheing in the course of time."[166] Athanasius argues that humanity was safe from dissolution and non-existence only through participation in the Logos, and thus could be saved only by virtue of the re-creative work of the Logos who figuratively came once again to sit for his portrait in the incarnation in order to renew his image in humanity.[167] "For being Word of the Father, and above all, he alone of natural fitness was both able to recreate everything, and worthy to suffer on behalf of all and to be ambassador for all with the Father."[168]

Over a century before Athanasius, Irenaeus emphasized the unity of creator and redeemer against the Gnostics and presented a distinctive view of atonement that has considerable promise for the doing of theology in a dynamic world. Irenaeus spoke of the work of Christ as *recapitulation.* The germ of this idea is found in the Gospels, where Jesus is pictured as in some ways repeating the history of Israel, or of humanity as a whole, but this time doing it correctly. The temptation narratives in the synoptics provide the clearest example. In Matthew and Luke Jesus is (as his quotations from Deuteronomy show) clearly going through the same testing that Israel experienced in the wilderness, but this time passing the tests. In Mark's briefer account, in which Jesus is "with the wild beasts," (Mark 1:13), the idea may be that he repeats the story of Adam in the Garden of Eden, where he named the animals that God created from the earth.

Irenaeus' idea is somewhat different. He pictures Jesus going through the whole course of a human life in order to save humanity at all stages.

For He came to save all through means of Himself—all, I say, who through Him are born again to God—infants, and children, and boys, and youths, and old men. He therefore passed through every age, becoming an infant for infants, thus sanctifying infants; a child for children, thus sanctifying those who are of this age, being at the same time made to them an example of piety, righteousness, and submission; a youth for youths, becoming an example to youths, and thus sanctifying them for the Lord. So likewise He was an old man for old men, that He might be a perfect Master for all, not merely as respects the setting forth of the truth, but also as regards age, sanctifying at the same time the aged also, and becoming an example to them likewise. Then, at last, He came on to death itself, that He might be "the first-born from the dead, that in all things He might have the pre-eminence," the Prince of life, existing before all, and going before all.[169]

(On the basis of John 8:57 Irenaeus argued that Jesus must have been over forty years old and thus in the second century could be said to have reached old age.)

In his study of the theology of Irenaeus, Wingren sets out the implications of this concept.

The content of the term *recapitulatio* is both rich and diverse. There is, for instance, the idea of a restoration of the original in the word, a purificatory movement pointing backwards to the first Creation. This restoration is accomplished in Jesus's struggle against the Devil in a conflict which repeats the history of Adam, but with the opposite outcome. The idea of a repetition is thus part of the conception of recapitulation, but in a modified form— modified, that is, by the idea of victory. But since man was a growing being before he became enslaved, and since he is not restored until he has begun again to progress towards his destiny, man's restoration in itself is more than a mere reversion to his original position. The word *recapitulatio* also contains the idea of perfection or consummation, for recapitulation means that man's growth is resumed and renewed. That man grows, however, is merely a different aspect of the fact that God creates.

Growth is always receptive in character, something derived from the source of life. Man's resumed growth is for this reason identical with the life which streams from Christ, the Head, to all believers. And Christ is the Creator's own creative Word, the "hand" by which God gives life to man.[170]

The concept of restoration of an original state of the world has to be abandoned in an evolutionary understanding of creation. We may, however, understand it as a process of being reoriented to God's original goal for creation. The value of Irenaeus' thought for this discussion lies then in the idea that "growth is resumed and renewed"—growth in the proper direction, toward the fulfillment of God's purpose for humanity and the world.

The Reorientation of History

The first eleven chapters of Genesis form the biblical prehistory. They probably contain some fragments of historical information like memories of Mesopotamian floods which were used in constructing an account of a cosmic deluge, but they are not anything like what we regard today as accurate history. We read them as theological statements about God's relationship with the world and with humans in particular, and the condition of early humanity. And as we observed in the previous chapter, that condition, from the story of the forbidden fruit through the Tower of Babel and the scattering of the nations, is one of "falling." The picture is of humanity, with a few exceptions like Enoch and Noah, moving away from God.

We can then say rather loosely that history in the Bible begins with Abraham. This certainly does not mean that everything from Genesis 12 on is "history as it really happened." There are duplicate accounts of the same event and some conflicts with what we know from secular sources. Some of the people in these stories are no doubt fictitious, and some of the events that are described did not really occur in space-time. But the stories are set in a definite historical period, the second and first millennia B.C., and in locations that we can usually identify. Characters in the stories are portrayed as real people and not just names in genealogies. Genesis 12 begins the history of God reconciling the world to Godself, a story of the development of faith and understanding within the culture of ancient Israel and the Christian community.[171]

God does that by acting among alienated human beings. "Long ago," Joshua later told the Israelites, "your ancestors—Terah and his sons Abraham and Nahor—lived beyond the Euphrates and served other gods" (Joshua 24:2). Abraham and his family could have been Exhibit A for Paul's indictment of humanity: "[T]hey exchanged the truth about God for a lie and worshipped and served the creature rather than the Creator, who is blessed forever!" (Romans 1:25).

It is in that setting that God calls the idolater Abram. There is nothing in the biblical story to suggest that he had greater insight than his pagan neighbors, no account like those of later Jewish legend and the Qur'an about how his astronomical observations led him to monotheism.[172] Without any preparation, rather like the way Jesus will later call disciples simply by saying "Follow me," the word comes to Abram.

> Go from your country and your kindred and your father's house to the land that I will show you. I will make of you a great nation, and I will bless you, and make your name great, so that you will be a blessing. I will bless those who bless you, and the one who curses you I will curse; and in you all the families of the earth shall be blessed (Genesis 12:1-3).

First, Abram is to be separated from his biological family. This separation is not absolute; later he will instruct his servant to go back to his relatives to get a wife for his son Isaac (Genesis 24:1-9). But even then, having Isaac remain in Canaan is given priority over marrying him to a member of his extended family (verses 6-8). The security of life within a tribe of biological relatives has to be foregone.

Then Abram is to be made "a great nation." That is expanded later in Genesis when God compares Abram's descendants with the stars of the sky (Genesis 15:5). Fulfillment of this promise would mean success in "the struggle for survival" of evolutionary biology. Abram's name is changed to Abraham, "father of a multitude" (Genesis 17:4 RSV), and he is pictured as having a total of eight sons by Hagar, Sarah, and finally Keturah. But as an indication of the relativizing of purely biological considerations, it is the one child of promise, Isaac, who is of importance for the ongoing biblical story. And the fact that his conception and birth come from an elderly couple who, by all normal standards for childbearing, are "as good as dead" (Romans 4:19) is a sign that God is involved in this birth in some special way.

If those first two aspects of the call of Abram relativize normal biological considerations, the third aspect transcends them. "In you all the families of the earth shall be blessed." The election of Abram and the promises made to him and his descendants are not just for that one biological group but ultimately for the sake of all the people of the world. Abram and his descendants are to benefit not just their own relatives but foreigners as well.

We are told a few verses later that when Abram reached Canaan "he built there an altar to the LORD, and invoked the name of the LORD" (Genesis 12:7). Here we are given no statement of abstract monotheism or confession of faith like the shema` of Deuteronomy 6:4. We simply are not told anything about how Abram may have thought about the relationship between YHWH and the gods of his ancestors or those of Canaan. We are told, however, that he worshipped *and trusted* the God who had called him. "He believed the LORD; and the LORD reckoned it to him as righteousness" (Genesis 15:6). That is why Paul would later celebrate him as "the ancestor of all who believe" (Romans 4:11).

At this stage of the biblical story and for some time thereafter the Hebrews apparently did not think that YHWH was the only God, but did believe that YHWH was the only God who should be worshipped —a type of belief referred to more precisely as henotheism. Monotheism in the strict sense doesn't emerge until the period of the exile, in Second Isaiah (e.g., Isaiah 45:18). Even the requirement that only YHWH be worshipped and that Israel should have "no other gods before me," as the First Commandment requires, seems to have been violated fairly often. We are told about the idolatry of Gideon (Judges 8:22-28) and Solomon (1 Kings 11:1-8) but not that they stopped worshipping YHWH. It was not easy for Israel to come to realize what it truly means to "love the LORD your God with all your heart, and with all your soul, and with all of your might" (Deuteronomy 6:5), as the long struggle of the prophets with the worship of the Canaanite Ba`als shows.

So while we should not dismiss the accounts of sudden revelatory breakthroughs granted to individuals like Abraham, Moses, and later prophets, Israelite religion had a slow historical development. We can call this evolution if we wish, but it was certainly not part of a generalized "Darwinian" process that operated by any type of survival of the fittest. There is no reason to think that a development from polytheism through henotheism to monotheism is "selected" by cultural forces alone, let alone by purely biological ones. That is not to say that biological and cultural influences had nothing to do with this development, and the belief that God acted through such influences is consistent with the idea that God generally works in the world by cooperating with creatures in their actions. But there is good reason to think that God was indeed active in guiding it in a distinctive way. That seems clear when we reflect on the character of the God in whom Israel was called to trust.

YHWH is identified in the Sinai theophany as the one "who brought you out of the land of Egypt, out of the house of slavery" (Exodus 20:2). The God of the Bible is the power who identified, in one of the great nations of the day, with some foreign slaves over against their imperial taskmasters and liberated them from bondage. "It was not because you were more numerous than any other people that the LORD set his heart on you and chose you—for you were the fewest of all peoples," Israel is told. "It was because the LORD loved you and kept the oath that he swore to your ancestors, that the LORD has brought you out with a mighty hand, and redeemed you from the house of slavery, from the hand of Pharaoh king of Egypt" (Deuteronomy 7:7-8). The idea that a small and oppressed people should be "chosen" rather than the great imperial power does have some similarities with the way biological evolution has worked, as Stephen Jay Gould emphasized—witness the demise of the dinosaurs and the rise of primates[173]—but it contradicts any simplistic idea of either biological or cultural selection.

The religious practices of Israel developed over the course of time. This can be seen, for example, in offering sacrifices, something for which there was a good deal of freedom in the early period but which later became more restricted. The regulation in Deuteronomy 12:13-14 limiting burnt offerings to "the place that the LORD will choose in one of your tribes" is put in the mouth of Moses, but the stories of Manoah and his wife (Judges 13:19) and Samuel (1 Samuel 7:9) indicate that in the pre-monarchic period Israelites might offer sacrifices wherever it was convenient. It was only later that the cult was centralized (at least as far as Judah was concerned) in Jerusalem. In addition, neither Manoah nor Samuel was of the tribe of Levi, let alone a member of the priestly family of Aaron. Again, the restriction of priestly functions to that family was apparently a later development.

In ethics, too, we can see development over the course of the biblical story. The unbounded vengeance expressed in the primitive song of Lamech (Genesis 4:23-24) is replaced by the "eye for eye" law of Exodus 21:23-24. Though that law is sometimes regarded as harsh, it in fact puts a limit on the retribution that can be demanded by an injured party. (That limit was no doubt not always observed in practice!) When Jesus later says that one should forgive seventy-seven times (Matthew 18:22) he is reversing Lamech's ancient demand for seventy-seven fold revenge.[174]

The fact that there is a development of ethical understanding within scripture can help us better understand some of the unpleasant aspects of the biblical story, such as the massacre of Canaanite populations described in the book of Joshua. That book as a whole, and these accounts of massacres in particular, are not straightforward historical reports. While the Israelites did no doubt engage in the "take no prisoners" practice of holy war in the ancient near east, it probably was not as systematic as these texts would indicate. Those accounts are more in the nature of what later writers and editors think *should* have been done to remove the possibility of religious syncretism with which they were quite familiar in Israel's later history. (This rationale is made clear in Deuteronomy 20:16-18.) The ongoing presence of non-Israelite populations in Canaan and the constant temptation for the people of Israel to adopt their religious practices shows on the one hand that the earlier populations were not wiped out and on the other hand that syncretism was an ongoing problem.

But we cannot deal with the ethical issue just by saying "This never happened." No doubt the Israelites did sometimes engage in the "Take no prisoners" practice of holy war in the ancient near east. The idea that God would command genocide should be disturbing to those who have learned the ethics of Jesus. Did God in fact command Israel to exterminate the Canaanites as a provisional measure? (We might compare what Jesus says about Moses allowing a man to divorce his wife in Mark 10:5.) Or did the Israelites engage in these practices because they thought that was the right way to serve a god and the Holy Spirit allowed the biblical writers to describe the situation in that way? We would then see again a divine accommodation to time-bound cultural concepts. It is of course tragic that some Christians have thought that these parts of scripture directed against the ancient Canaanites justified the same kind of treatment of Native Americans and other peoples.

The elimination of people foreign to the tribe can of course be the crudest expression of "survival of the fittest" in biological evolution. The attempt to get rid of foreign religious practices can be seen as a way of preserving the tribe's culture. But the theological concept of Israel as God's chosen people was not fundamentally a matter of biology (i.e., of genetics as the basis of election). A superficial reading of scripture may give the impression of a demand for "racial purity," but references to a "mixed crowd" (Exodus 12:38) and "rabble" (Numbers 11:4) with Israel in the Exodus, as well as the stories of Rahab and the Gibeonites during the conquest (Joshua 2:1-21; 6:22-25; and 9:1-27) form a subtext indicating that such purity was sometimes not a concern. It is not until the return of the Jews from the Babylonian exile, when the community around Jerusalem was a small group surrounded by hostile neighbors, that we find in the books of Ezra and Nehemiah protests against mixed marriages and insistence that the purity of the "holy seed" (Ezra 9:2) be protected. The book of Ruth, whose heroine is repeatedly referred to as "the Moabitess" [hamo'abhiyah], was probably intended to counter that emphasis.

The prophets of Israel apparently had little interest in biological purity. They are much more interested in loyalty to YHWH alone as well as issues of social justice. They display a clear precedence of cultural over biological development, something that is especially manifest in the universal outlook of the great but nameless prophet of Second Isaiah. Here God calls his servant Israel to be "a light to the nations, that my salvation may reach to the end of the earth" (Isaiah 49:6), picking up the theme of the promise to Abraham that all the families of the earth would be blessed in him.

The purpose of pointing out these developments in the religion of Israel is not to impose an alien evolutionary scheme on the Bible. The fact that there were historical developments in the beliefs, worship, and ethics of the Israelites is clear from scripture itself as long as we do not force our preconceptions on the text. Abraham, Moses, David, and other Old Testament figures did not know God as Trinity, did not have an expectation of a crucified Messiah, and did not think of the Passover as prefiguring the Lord's Supper. What they did know were the difficulties of their lives and the hopes given to them by God's promises.

Some of those promises took the form of a royal Messiah, a righteous king from the family of David (Jeremiah 23:5-6) or a new Moses (Deuteronomy 18:15-22). Those promises were brief and not terribly specific, and consequently could be filled in by the faithful with whatever they thought would solve the problems of their people. Psalm 72 was given the superscription, "A Psalm of Solomon," but neither the real Solomon nor any of the other kings of Judah and Israel were more than pale reflections of the king pictured there. (Isaac Watts would later paraphrase this psalm in his hymn, "Jesus shall reign where'er the sun".[175]) During the time of the oppressive Roman occupation that began in the last century B.C., the messianic expectation not surprisingly took on nationalistic coloring. But with the possible exception of the writer of the fourth servant song of Isaiah (52:13—53:12), very few in Israel expected that God's promises would be fulfilled as they were in the career of the carpenter Jesus of Nazareth.

CHAPTER VI

THE TURNING POINT

The Coming of God

God's work of reorienting the course of creation, begun with the call of Abraham and continuing in the history of Israel, comes to its critical point in the Israelite Jesus of Nazareth: "When the fullness of time had come, God sent his Son, born of a woman, born under the law, in order to redeem those who were under the law, so that we might receive adoption as children" (Galatians 4:4-5). Paul does not try to explain what made the time of Jesus' birth the right time. We can speculate about that as long as we do not allow our guesses to get in the way of the positive affirmations scripture does make about the sending of God's Son.

Rome had established an empire over the known world that, oppressive as it was for many of its people, did make travel and communications possible over much of Europe, northern Africa, and the Middle East. The Greek philosophical tradition was already being used by Jews and soon would be adopted by Christian apologists and theologians. Even though there was a significant amount of anti-Jewish sentiment in parts of the empire, Judaism was a recognized religion in Roman law and was in the process of becoming a world religion. The number of "God fearers" (Gentiles who were friendly to Judaism and attended synagogue but—for males—were not circumcised) and proselytes (cf. Matthew 23:15 and Acts 2:10) was significant. The scriptures of Israel had been translated into the Greek that many people spoke, so that they were available to Gentiles. All of these factors could be seen as preparation for the birth of the one God sent to reconcile the world to Godself.

The developments that were sketched at the end of the last chapter indicate that there was some continuity between what God had been doing in the previous history of Israel and what God would now do in and through Jesus. The Hebrew scriptures can be described as the story of "the Word becoming flesh."[176] What God had been doing in the rest of the world cannot be neglected either. Greeks and Romans come on the biblical scene, or at least are in the wings, in the intertestamental period in 1 and 2 Maccabees. While we need not regard developments of philosophy and religion in non-Jewish cultures as revelatory in the same sense as events in the history of Israel, they still may be understood as, in differing degrees, preparations for the gospel mission. The influence of the Persian faith of Zoroastrianism on Judaism during the intertestamental period, for example, should be noted.[177]

At the same time the one we focus on now is, as Paul affirmed in that verse from Galatians, the Son of God. The continuity of God's action in world history has to be understood together with the fact that God now comes into the world in a novel way, "perpendicularly from above" (*senkrecht von oben*) as Karl Barth put it.[178] This is simply to say that Jesus Christ is fully God as well as fully human. While in his humanity he is fully a part of the evolutionary history of the cosmos, distantly related to all extant and extinct terrestrial species like the rest of humanity, his divinity is something novel and unique. Humanity does not evolve to divinity, but evolution is part of the process—a process in which God has been at work throughout—by which God comes into the world as Jesus of Nazareth.

How could God's horizontal and vertical actions come together in one person who is genuinely human and fully divine? The Definition of Chalcedon[179] has been the church's authoritative statement about this since the fifth century. It should, however, be seen not primarily as an answer to the question of *how* Jesus can be both God and human but as a statement of boundaries for thinking about who Jesus is. Christians are "to acknowledge one and the same Son, our Lord Jesus Christ, at once complete in Godhead and complete in manhood, truly God and truly man." This is not to say that the "how" issue is of no importance, but it is a second order question.

This can best be appreciated if we take seriously the fundamental claim of our theology, that God is most fully revealed in the event of the cross: "True theology and recognition of God are in the crucified Christ." Historically Israel knew God as the one who created them as a people in the Exodus. That knowledge of God is still valid, but in the light of the cross-resurrection event our relationship with God and understanding of who God is now begins with the Crucified One who is risen. Through him we know the one to whom he prayed as Father and their mutual Spirit. That is a first order confession of faith.

But Jesus began his public ministry proclaiming that the reign of God was near, not by saying, "I am God." There was nothing about his appearance to make his contemporaries think that he was divine. He was born, circumcised, got hungry and thirsty and tired, suffered, and died. He came, not as an abstraction, some kind of unfallen humanity, but "in the likeness of sinful flesh" (Romans 8:3). God "made him to be sin who knew no sin, so that in him we might become the righteousness of God" (2 Corinthians 5:21).

The traditional Western understandings of original sin and sin of origin posed a christological problem: How could Christ be the sinless Son of God if he, like all other people, shared in this hereditary condition? Solving that problem was one of the motivations behind the Roman Catholic teaching that at her conception Mary had been kept free of original guilt by anticipation of the merits of Christ. Because of that her son could receive unfallen human nature from her. There is, however, no "gene for original sin" that is transmitted biologically from parents to children. The human problem, as I have argued, is a combination of the fact that we have biological *tendencies* for behaviors that, in some circumstances, can be sinful *and* that from the beginnings of our lives we are in a toxic cultural environment. "In the likeness of sinful flesh," Jesus shared that condition, as the Orthodox tradition has generally held.[180] The New Testament affirms in a number of places (e.g., 1 Peter 2:22), however, that he did not actually commit sin. As Barth put it, "'Without sin' means that in our human and sinful existence as a man He did not sin."[181]

How could that be? One might be tempted to answer that sin was impossible for him since he was God incarnate, and we certainly have to take seriously the claim that he is not simply human but the Son of God as human. But that should not be understood to mean that this gave Jesus a kind of invincible armor against sin, for that would effectively deny that he had a human will and would reduce his temptations (including the final one, to come down from the cross) to a charade. It was the human Jesus, one "made like his brothers and sisters in every respect" (Hebrews 2:17 RSV) who did not sin.

He was also the one whose conception came about when the Holy Spirit overshadowed Mary (Luke 1:35), whose ministry began with the descent of the Spirit and was carried out in the power of that same Spirit (Luke 3:22, 4:1, 14, and 18). We cannot get inside Jesus' experience and really know how he thought about the temptations that faced him or how he felt about them. How he was able to keep from sinning must remain to some extent a mystery to us. But from the standpoint of faith it seems reasonable to suggest that the Holy Spirit, who has sometimes been described as the "bond of love" between Father and Son in the Trinity, made it possible for the incarnate Son to remain faithful to the Father against all the trials and enticements that were thrown at him. In fact, the question of how this one "in the likeness of sinful flesh" could avoid sin forces us to appreciate the fully trinitarian character of the incarnation.[182]

And it is this same Spirit who is given to believers because of Jesus' death and resurrection, as John (19:30; 20:22) and Acts (2:1-4) picture in different ways. In fact, (as we will discuss in the next chapter), it is the Holy Spirit who enables them to *be* believers. The freedom from sin of God's new creation is an eschatological hope which the Spirit gives to believers today (Romans 8:1-17).

A Life of Reconciliation

Now look around you, across the wide world
And above you, at oceans and the great hanging
Arch of the sky—see how Heaven's
King comes to you, longing for His death.[183]

These lines, addressed by an Anglo-Saxon poet to Jerusalem, give one answer to the question, "Why did God become human?" He did so in order to die: "The Son of man *must* (*dei*) undergo great suffering, and be rejected by the elders, the chief priests, and the scribes, and be killed" (Mark 8:31, emphasis added). It is no accident that the creeds move immediately from Jesus' birth to his suffering and death "under Pontius Pilate" and resurrection, for God's assumption of our human condition and his death and defeat of death are the heart of salvation.

And yet the entire life of Jesus and what other views of atonement have called his "active obedience" cannot be neglected. (Christ saves us "by the whole course of his obedience," Calvin said.[184]) The life of Christ sets down in the midst of a sinful world a real instance of reconciliation with God, for Jesus' life, as the gospels present it to us, is one of complete trust in, and obedience to, the Father. Flowing from that trust and obedience it is a life that displays love of neighbor in the sense portrayed for us by the parable of the Good Samaritan.

Jesus' acceptance of sinners was a work of new creation, and his table fellowship with them—a fellowship that laid the groundwork for the Christian community's celebration of the Lord's Supper—shows what that new creation is to be. His healings of the sick (however we understand those cures to have taken place) were signs, not of a return to a golden age (which never existed) in which there was no disease, but of God's intended future for creation. (It is no accident, as we noted earlier, that so many of the gospel stories of these healings were on the Sabbath.) Atonement is not simply a display of power or something that God does to get his own property back but a self-giving act for the benefit of creation.

The Nicene and Apostles' Creeds move immediately from Jesus' birth to his passion, death, and resurrection, with no mention of his intervening ministry. On the other hand, the early Christian teaching about Jesus summarized in Peter's address to Cornelius and his household includes the words "he went about doing good" (Acts 10:38). A phrase like that might well have been included in the creeds. Some people might want such an expansion of the creed in order to emphasize Jesus' role as teacher, miracle worker, or social reformer at the expense of his cross and resurrection. Against any such attempts, the event of the cross must maintain a central role in Christian confessions, but criticism of the creeds because of their omission of anything about Jesus' life and ministry is not a "fairly silly objection."[185] It is simply an observation that the one who was born of Mary, who died on the cross and rose on the third day, should be identified by something more than a name. To say something like "he went about doing good" is to define, in a very brief way, his character and work. And since Jesus is God's revelation of what humanity is supposed to be, a concise statement of that sort tells us what we are saved *for*.

Some of Jesus' contemporaries thought that he was the Messiah, although he himself seems (as in Mark 8:30) to have discouraged such talk. But there was another way in which Jews could express a belief that Jesus was a fulfillment of God's promises to Israel, one that he is never said to have turned down. We are told that after the feeding of the 5,000 the people exclaimed, "This is indeed the prophet who is to come into the world" (John 6:14). Also, when Jesus entered Jerusalem on Passion Sunday "the crowds were saying, 'This is the prophet Jesus from Nazareth in Galilee'" (Matthew 21:11). Jesus' teaching was an essential part of his work, one that for many of his contemporaries put him in the same class as the prophets of old.

Prophets were in short supply in Israel at Jesus' time. The common understanding was that prophecy had ceased long before. The word of God no longer came as it had to people like Amos, Huldah, or Ezekiel.[186] But John the Baptist was considered a prophet by many of the people (Mark 11:32 and parallels), and that apparently seemed to be a good way for people to think of someone who made the impression that Jesus did as well. Jesus' teaching was fully in the tradition of the older prophets of Israel: denunciations of unfaithfulness to the covenant and social injustice, calls for repentance, and promises of the coming decisive action of God to do away with evil and bring righteousness. Regarded simply as a prophet, he did not teach anything that differed qualitatively from the messages of Isaiah or Jeremiah.

And yet Jesus was seen as more than just another prophet. One of the popular titles that the Baptist refused was "the prophet" (John 1:21), the reference being to the promise attributed to Moses in Deuteronomy 18:15: "The LORD your God will raise up for you a prophet like me from among your own people, you shall heed such a prophet." With the absence of prophets in the intertestamental period (cf. 1 Maccabees 4:46), this promise had taken on a significance comparable with that of the hope for a Messiah. In fact, the verse from John 6 reporting that the crowd thought that Jesus was the prophet promised by Moses is followed by Jesus withdrawing because he "realized that they were about to come and take him by force to make him king" (John 6:15). The Samaritans, descendants of those who long ago had rejected the Davidic dynasty, did not look for a Davidic Messiah. Their hope was for the prophet like Moses, "the one who returns." Presumably that is translated into Judaic terms in John 4:25.[187]

The popular idea of the biblical prophets as primarily long-range forecasters is wrong. As one adage has it, they were more "forth tellers" than "foretellers." But they certainly did sometimes speak of what God would do in the future, and by the time of Jesus the genre of apocalyptic, whose earlier stages we find in Old Testament prophets like Zechariah, got a great deal of attention. It is hardly surprising then that, as a man of his culture, Jesus would have adopted this form of speech at times, as Mark 13 and its parallels indicate that he did.

But the most distinctive of the statements about the future that are attributed to Jesus in the gospels are the three synoptic "passion predictions" (Mark 8:31; 9:31; and 10:32-34 and parallels). Critical scholars tend to see these as predictions after the event, formulated in the light of Easter by the church, and this may well be true of many of the details of these statements. However, there is nothing at all impossible even on a purely human level about a prophet who had already provoked opposition from the religious establishment and who could be seen as a challenge to Roman rule knowing the probability of his arrest and execution in Jerusalem. It is even less surprising if Jesus really is the Son of God.

But resurrection? The term "passion prediction" is really too narrow for the verses mentioned in the previous paragraph since they (with the exception of Luke 9:44) also include references to rising on the third day. We should also take into account the reports of Jesus' statement about destroying the temple and raising it up (John 2:19; Mark 14:58; Matthew 26:61), whose occurrence in John and the synoptic tradition in varying forms suggests an authentic basis.

Again there is nothing impossible within the Jewish tradition about Jesus expressing belief in a general resurrection. Resurrection of the dead as an eschatological event was a tenet of the Pharisees, and Jesus' exchange with the Sadducees (Mark 12:18-27 and parallels) shows that he believed it as well. This Pharisaic belief did not envision the resurrection of one individual before the end of history, but the study by Pinchas Lapide indicates that it would have been possible for a Jew to accept that idea.[188] However, Jesus' expression of a belief that he would be raised after crucifixion would not be the same type of thing as expectation of his condemnation and death. The latter could be guessed by a disinterested observer who knew the ways of the world, but belief in one's resurrection could be held, humanly speaking, only as an expression of trust in the faithfulness of God.

The prophets of Israel did not just talk. Sometimes they would dramatize their message in "action prophecies," like the smashing of an earthenware jug by Jeremiah (19:1-14) to picture the destruction that God would bring on Jerusalem because of its unfaithfulness. The prophet's own life could become such a prophecy, as when the death of Ezekiel's wife ("Mortal, with one blow I am about to take away from you the delight of your eyes") became a sign of judgment on the city (Ezekiel 24:15-27). In that tradition, the cross-resurrection event can be seen as the ultimate action prophecy.

The Cross-Resurrection Event as Fiducial Influence

"Then, at last," as Irenaeus says, "He came on to death itself."[189] Jesus' proclamation of the nearness of the Kingdom of God would have been seen by Roman officials in Judea as a challenge to their rule, and both the Sadducean priests and the Pharisees had been criticized by him. It is no surprise that they all wanted him out of the way. But the death he came to was one that, at least in the short term, Jesus could have avoided. As he and his disciples went out from supper on that Thursday night he could have said to them, "It's too hot for me here. We'd better get out of town." And by morning they would have been into the wilderness or across the Jordan. He didn't do that, however, but turned aside to Gethsemane.

So we come to the question, what did his death accomplish? Why was it "according to the definite plan and foreknowledge of God" (Acts 2:23)? How does it bring about atonement between God and humanity?

Reconciliation worth talking about must be something that takes place between God and people in the real world. That does not mean that metaphorical statements of its meaning and even mythic images of how it is accomplished are of no value, but they cannot be given a primary position. Gerhard Forde's treatment of the work of Christ has precisely the merit of emphasizing this real character of atonement over against more abstract views.[190] Atonement, he argued, must be an "actual event,"[191] something that really gets rid of the separation between God and humanity that has been caused by the fundamental sin of idolatry.

As we have seen, theologians through the centuries have produced a number of theories of the atonement, and there have been extensive debates about them. Forde made an important point that relativizes the importance of those discussions: "For theories do not reconcile," he emphasized. "If dogmatics covers the offense with its theories, it cannot serve a proclamation that actually *is* a ministry of reconciliation."[192] What saves us is the life, death, and resurrection of Christ as they come to us in Word and sacraments. We are not saved by theories about how those things work to bring about atonement, however good those theories may be.

That point may seem obvious and even trivial. The map is not the territory and a recipe in a cookbook is not a meal. But Forde's statement is more than a generality. Theories of the atonement have often assumed or set up theological systems that specify various things that supposedly have to be done in order for God and humanity to be reconciled. A debt had to be paid, either to God or the devil. The divine honor, offended by human sin, had to be restored. Retributive justice demands that there be punishment for evildoers. Satan has to be tricked into giving up his prey. The tyrants that hold humanity captive must be defeated. Cultic requirements must be fulfilled. All of these may, within limits, be useful metaphors for certain purposes, but they tend to obscure the fact that what actually gets the job done is the life of Jesus of Nazareth, his death on a criminal's cross, and his resurrection. Atonement is not first of all a matter of conformity to any theological system. It is a matter of the cross-resurrection event actually doing something to people—of it being an "actual event."

But what kind of event needs to take place? Atonement is necessary because God and humanity are not "at one." We have separated ourselves from God by our fundamental sin of refusal to trust in God. That trust is the basic thing for which the First Commandment calls, as Luther explains in the Large Catechism. What does it mean to say that we are to have no other gods than the one who brought Israel out of Egypt? "A 'god'," Luther says, "is the term for that to which we are to look for all good and in which we are to find refuge in all need. Therefore, to have a god is nothing else than to trust and believe in that one with your whole heart."[193] In Romans 1:18-31 Paul sees the fact that humans failed to trust first in God, but instead "worshipped and served the creature rather than the Creator" as the root of the human problem, the source of all other sins, and the reason why "the wrath of God is revealed from heaven."

In other words, there is a fundamental lack of faith in the true God. This is not simply an absence of knowledge about certain facts or failure to assent to certain doctrinal claims, but a lack of confidence in and reliance on the proper object of faith, our creator. This may be a nihilistic lack of trust in anything, but it is more likely a placing of ultimate trust in things that are not God. Since that is the problem, the solution must be creation of genuine faith in the real God. God must act in a way that brings idolaters to abandon their false faiths and put their trust in the one who is the source of their lives, the God revealed in Christ. Idolatrous faith must be eliminated, and genuine faith must be restored. And when that happens, the wrath of God can come to an end since there is then no longer any cause for it.

"If you feel distant from God, guess who moved" is an expression of popular theology. The reason that atonement is needed is that we humans have alienated ourselves from our creator, not vice versa. Atonement means that we are brought back to where we belong. This does not mean that atonement has no effect on God. The divine wrath is indeed brought to an end. But it is ended because our faith in God is restored, not because legal or cultic requirements were fulfilled. In particular, God's wrath does not need to be assuaged by meeting some prior conditions *before* God is willing to be merciful to us. By bringing people to faith, God expresses the divine mercy and simultaneously does away with divine wrath.

The critical question then is how faith can come about. It is not simply a matter of convincing people of the truth of certain religious claims. The crucial aspect of "saving faith" in the Christian sense is trust in the true God. The old scholastic tripartite analysis of faith has at least some limited value. It distinguished *notitia* (knowledge of what is to be believed), *assensus* (assent that what is to be believed is true), and *fiducia* (trust in the object of faith).[194] This can too easily give the impression that saving faith is a matter of agreeing to the truth of doctrinal propositions, but that danger can be avoided. In order for one to have genuine faith in God one must know and believe that the true God is the one revealed in the history of Israel that culminates in the cross-resurrection event and, most crucially, place one's trust in that God. The latter element, *fiducia,* is what is really essential.

Atonement happens when all our idols are dethroned and true faith in the true God is created. And that is what the cross and resurrection of Jesus accomplish. This is, first of all, God's "alien work" of condemnation and destruction.[195] Our trust in false gods, in our religious, political, and moral systems and our own selves, must be exposed and discredited. And this happens when we realize that these idolatries have killed the source of our life. Of course the cross did not come upon God as a surprise, but it was not God who cried, "Crucify him." It was humans like ourselves, through our representatives among the religious leaders in Jerusalem and the Roman political authorities, who demanded and carried out the crucifixion of Jesus.

If we are honest we have to say that we can see their point. They could give plausible reasons why somebody doing and saying the things that Jesus did and said had to be eliminated. People concerned about religion and morality knew that you couldn't just freely forgive sinners. After all, there had to be some standards and some requirements for people to be considered righteous, or else the whole religious system would collapse. Those with political authority realized that even though Jesus might not have offered any open challenge to them, such a challenge was implicit in talk about the first being last and the last first as well as pointing to some kind of kingdom other than that of Caesar. Economic stability was threatened by someone who told people to give away their wealth and who attacked a respectable currency exchange. And when Jesus failed to seize the opportunity to raise the standard of revolt against Rome as the crowds were acclaiming him with palms when he rode into Jerusalem, the freedom fighters thought that he had betrayed the revolution. Give us Barabbas!

Or we may sympathize with those who were afraid to speak up against an unjust execution, or those who just didn't want to get involved. Sometimes the sensible course of action, the one that keeps us out of trouble, is to keep quiet and not get involved. Jesus' story of the Good Samaritan is a challenge to get involved, in spite of the trouble and danger that it might bring. Perhaps it would have made no difference in the end if the disciples had not run away in Gethsemane and if Peter had not denied that he knew Jesus. But we are called to be on God's side whether or not that seems to be the prudent thing to do.

The fact is that the message Jesus proclaimed and the things he did get in the way of the personal agendas and the visions for the world of normal people. What sensible person could consider "Those who love their life lose it, and those who hate their life in this world will keep it for eternal life" (John 12:25) to be good counsel? So, with the approval of Caiaphas, Pilate had Jesus put to death. And it was no "death with dignity." Crucifixion was the most humiliating and agonizing death that the ancient world could devise, a death that Torah (Deuteronomy 21:23) considered accursed. For Jesus it was a God-forsaken death (Mark 15:34 and Matthew 27:46), seemingly one that showed his idea of having a special relationship with God and his whole mission to have been tragically misguided. By the standards of normal people, that was the end of the story.

But then Jesus was reported to have been raised from the dead, and to have appeared to the disciples, who had abandoned him, saying, "Peace be with you" (John 20:19-21). His disciples quickly came to believe that this showed Jesus to be the Son of God (Romans 1:4) and even simply "God" (John 20:28). If the claim of the resurrection is true it means at a minimum that God has acted for Jesus and vindicated him.

If that is really the case then we are forced see the inevitable end of all false faiths, all the illusions cherished by ourselves and others who have grown up acculturated to sin. Jesus died "for us" because we had to get rid of him to preserve our systems and projects that were challenged by his life and words. Jesus Christ is what humanity was always intended to be, so humanity that has turned away from God and refuses to be what God intended killed him. That means that the cross is the destruction of humanity, the end of sinners. When we are brought to understand this, we realize that the idols upon which we depended and which motivated our behavior work death rather than life. They cannot be trusted. And when the objects of our deepest faith are seen to be lies, in a real sense we die.

God has allowed us to kill our one real hope, the union of God with humanity, as the end of our self-chosen road. This alien work is foreign to God's loving character, but it is work that must be done in order for true faith to be possible. Only if our false faith is shattered can we be brought to see that we cannot put our ultimate trust in ourselves or any other creature.

And the cross-resurrection event is saving grace. When we are brought to see that our true creator was willing to die for us, indeed *did* die for us, and comes back announcing peace, then we will be convinced that God is trustworthy "above all things." This is God's "proper work," bringing about true faith and reconciliation with the God who "justifies the ungodly . . . gives life to the dead and calls into existence the things that do not exist" (Romans 4:5, 17). And when true faith arises, God's wrath comes to an end. We are, as Paul says, "dead to sin and alive to God" (Romans 6:11).

The fact that reconciliation takes place when people come to faith enables us to answer the question that has been asked so often about other ideas of atonement: Why can't God just forgive sinners without Jesus having to die? Presumably God could do that, but there would then be no reconciliation because there would be no genuine faith. For God to write off sin as a bad debt, so to speak, would amount to God simply letting humanity continue to move away from God's intended goal. It would mean that God accepted the failure of creation.

But God has acted to reconcile sinners to Godself by bringing them to faith through the event of the cross. Those who have this faith are "in Christ," and Paul says of them in 2 Corinthians 5:17 that each one is "a new creation." It is by bringing people to faith through the cross-resurrection event that God begins the work of reorienting the course of creation toward the goal described in Ephesians 1:10.

The "if" and "when" qualifications in the previous paragraphs raise some important questions. What about reconciliation of those who have never been encountered by the cross-resurrection message, and have not then had the opportunity to see in it the destruction of their idols and the God in whom true faith may be placed? That is, of course, a classic challenge to Christianity, and it will be addressed in the final chapter. And what about those who have heard this message but who, like some on Mars Hill, "scoffed" (Acts 17:32)? Why do some believe while others don't? That is another old problem about which Christians have disagreed, and the present approach does not seem to offer any fresh light on it. The discussion of the scope of atonement in the final chapter is, however, relevant to it.

The historic cross and resurrection of Jesus under Pontius Pilate was an actual event, but it becomes the event that reconciles each one of us when it we are encountered by the reality of the cross and resurrection—when we are addressed by the word of the cross. "Faith comes from what is heard, and what is heard comes through the word of Christ" (Romans 10:17). That word must encounter us in Spirit-empowered proclamation if it is to work real atonement. This again makes it clear that theories about how atonement works are of secondary importance. Models and metaphors of atonement can be helpful, but they do not take the place of the fact itself. The fundamental task of preaching is to proclaim God's work of reconciliation. As one pastor put it, "I have only one sermon: 'Come, sinners, and look on Christ!'"[196]

Theories of the atonement are not without value, however. The development of adequate theories is part of the theological task of "faith in search of understanding." The proclamation of Christ sets out the central Christian claim that the events of Good Friday and Easter reconcile us with God. If someone then asks, "How does that work?" we need to have a theory, whether formal or informal, if we are to give an adequate answer. A theory does not atone, but it can help atonement to be understood as part of the whole Christian view of creation and salvation and our relationship with the world, and thus aid in sustaining intelligent faith. The fundamental purpose of any theology, including its theory of the atonement, is to support the proclamation of law and gospel.

A good theoretical description of the event of atonement that has been sketched here can start with what Knutson described as the "magnet" picture of atonement.[197] That image is based on Jesus' words in John 12:32: "And I, when I am lifted up from the earth, will draw all people to myself." Knutson used that language in his discussion of "moral influence" theories that go back at least to Abelard. The basic idea of such theories has usually been that the love of God shown by Christ's willingness to die for sinners evokes corresponding love from us. As 1 John 4:19 puts it, "We love because he first loved us." This mutual love is then supposed to mean that we have been reconciled to God.

These theories are often characterized as "subjective," but that may not be an accurate description. A theory of this type can argue that the cross of Christ actually does something objective, exerting a real influence on God as well as on people and thus bringing them to a loving condition. The problem with moral influence theories is not that they have to be entirely subjective. Nor is the problem that they speak of a change in the human person rather than a change in God's attitude. As we have already seen, God's wrath really is done away with when we are reconciled. The basic difficulty with theories of Abelard's type is rather that we are not justified by love but by faith (Romans 3:28; Ephesians 2:8).

The approach that Forde presented and that I have followed in the preceding discussion can be called a theory not of *moral* influence but of *fiducial* influence.[198] What the cross-resurrection event does is first destroy idolatrous faith and then create genuine faith in the true God. We are turned around in our flight from God and brought back toward the goal that God has always intended, the union of creatures with their creator. That is what reconciliation is all about.

Giving the label "fiducial influence" to the view described here may help to get this view considered along with other theories that bear familiar labels like "Christus Victor" or "penal substitution." It is, after all, hard to discuss a theory that has no name. (Forde was content to call it "atonement as actual event," but it seems best to be explicit about what the actual event does.[199]) And the name "fiducial influence" has the merit of emphasizing two critical features.

First of all, we are justified by faith, *fiducia*. While all parts of the church confess that faith is essential for salvation, it is actually secondary in most other theories of the atonement. We have already seen that the usual "moral influence" theories make the mistake of putting their emphasis on love rather than faith. And it is true that Anselm, after describing the way in which the death of Christ satisfies the divine honor, represents God as saying to the sinner, "Receive my only-begotten Son, and give him for yourself" to "call us and draw us to the Christian faith."[200] But nothing is said there about faith as trust in God's promise or about the work of atonement as being directed toward the creation of faith. Nor does the Christus Victor theory require any attention to faith. (The index of Aulén's book has no entries for the word.) With fiducial influence, on the other hand, atonement is achieved precisely when people are brought to faith— that is, to trust in the true God revealed in Christ.

And secondly, saving faith is not something that we can call up by ourselves. If it were, then it could be considered a good work for which we could claim credit in God's sight. It is indeed our faith—for it is human beings who are brought to trust in God's promise—but we have it only as a result of a divine influence upon us. We will discuss that point further in the next chapter.

The operative influence is, as Abelard said, the love of God displayed in the event of the cross. "The love of God does not first discover but creates what is pleasing to it," Luther said in the last of the "paradoxes" in which he set out his theology of the cross.[201] This work of new creation follows the pattern of the divine *creatio ex nihilo*. It is indeed God's love shown in the event of the cross that brings this about. Human love for God does result from this, but as far as atonement is concerned that is a secondary effect. It is the creation of faith that is crucial.

The Descent of the Creator

We have, then, a relatively straightforward description of the way God creates a new humanity by bringing people to faith. There is another way to speak of this, not in opposition to the previous approach but with language that is more dramatic and pictorial. Its utility is not so much in systematic theology as in furnishing images for proclamation. Here we focus on the idea that Christ descends into the *nihil*, the nothingness that denies creation, so that God can again create *ex nihilo*. Symbolically it is Christ's combat with the devil, whose speech in Goethe's *Faust* represents him as the enemy of God's creation:

I am the Spirit that ever denies!
And justly so; for all that's born
Deserves to be destroyed in scorn.
Therefore 'twere best if nothing were created![202]

The Apostles' Creed states unambiguously that Jesus was "crucified, dead, and buried." Then, before saying that he rose on the third day, it continues with the last phrase to become part of this confession of faith, *descendit ad inferna*. Even the translation of this phrase is debated. The traditional rendering is "He descended into hell," while the version of the International Consultation on English texts is "He descended to the dead."[203]

Although the traditional translation suggests richer imagery, the modern one is not a mere banality. The redundancy, if indeed it is that, of saying "crucified, dead, and buried. He descended to the dead" means "He really did die. It is no figure of speech." (Compare the repetition of phrases emphasizing the divinity of the Son in the Nicene Creed.) We should not allow descent to the dead to be colored by speculations about the afterlife that envision the souls of the departed as being immediately in heaven, for the Hebrew picture is more stark. In Sheol, the common grave of humanity, no one can praise God (Psalm 6:5) and the dead are forgotten by him (Psalm 88:5.)

The traditional English translation of the Apostles' Creed, however, has "he descended into hell." The early church and medieval Christians believed that Christ had descended into Hades to announce the defeat of the powers of evil and liberate the saints of the Old Testament. This "harrowing of hell" was once a common literary theme, the fourteenth century English poem "Piers the Ploughman" being a good example.[204] The typical Orthodox icon of the resurrection shows the risen Christ who has broken down the gates of hell, trampling Satan underfoot and releasing Adam and others from prison.[205]

A number of biblical texts have been cited in support of this idea of Christ's descent into hell, but the relevance of all of them is open to some question. One text that is commonly cited is 1 Peter 3:18-20, which says that, after having been "made alive in the spirit," Christ "went and made a proclamation to the spirits in prison." There is, however, no reference to "descent" or mention of the defeat of Satan.[206]

Luther introduced a radically different idea. He saw Christ's true "descent into hell" in his passion and the God-forsakenness on the cross that wrenched the cry, "My God, my God, why have you forsaken me?" (Mark 15:34; Matthew 27:46) from him. That cry is not to be explained away by saying, for example, that Jesus was pointing to the fulfillment of prophecy! If Psalm 22:1 is indeed prophetic in that sense, it predicts one who truly feels forsaken by God. And if God indeed "made him to be sin" (2 Corinthians 5:21), then he suffered the ultimate consequence of sin, hell.[207]

The Reformed tradition has generally understood Christ's descent into hell in that way. The descent into hell is then seen as the depths of Christ's passion, and Barth developed this idea at some length in *Church Dogmatics*.[208] The Roman Catholic Hans Urs von Balthasar, on the other hand, developed a theology of Holy Saturday that emphasized Christ's "going to the dead" that followed his physical death but still in a sense was part of his passion. Balthasar's ideas have been subjected to detailed criticism, with defense of the traditional Roman Catholic view, by Pitstick.[209]

The idea of Luther and the Reformed tradition that Christ's descent into hell should be understood as the depth of his suffering rather than a transition to a place of the dead is usually part of an understanding of atonement as penal substitution. Christ in his passion experienced the pains of the damned. But there is another emphasis that can be given to it. On Calvary the creator enters into the lowest and most humiliating end. He suffers what was considered the worst kind of death, one designed to display its victim as a complete failure deserving only of horror and mockery. The cry that God had abandoned him meant that he was dying in separation from the source of life, in the darkness where God cannot find God. Yet it was the person of the Son of God, the one through whom all things were made, who cried out. By taking on human dying, God goes into the deep, the nothingness that threatens creation.

Besides holding the view that has just been described, Luther also maintained—partly because the creed mentions the descent after the death and burial—that Christ did descend victoriously to the place of the dead to show his victory over sin and death. That is the position of the later Lutheran Formula of Concord, which included a lengthy excerpt from one of Luther's sermons to this effect.[210]

With the approach to atonement that we are pursuing here, those two views of the descent into hell—the nadir of the passion and in a sense the first act of the resurrection—need not be seen as mutually exclusive. Atonement as new creation parallels God's original creative act, for by taking on human dying, God has entered into the nothingness that threatens creation, in order to renew creation. Recall Bonhoeffer's statement: "The fact that Christ was dead did not provide the possibility of his resurrection but its impossibility; it was nothing itself, it was *nihil negativum*. There is absolutely no transition, no continuum between the dead Christ and the resurrected Christ, but the freedom of God that in the beginning created God's work out of nothing." [211]

This work of re-creation is not something that God does for God's own benefit. (It is not, for example, to be seen simply as the rescue of the Son by the Father.) It is the work of atonement, restoring creation by rescuing it from the hopelessness and ultimate annihilation of separation from God. A popular American television series of a few years ago provides an illustration that, if used with some care, can be instructive. "Prison Break" in later seasons moved on to other plots but its original idea was suggestive. A man has been wrongly convicted of murder and sent to prison. In order to free him, his brother deliberately gets convicted of a crime so that he can get into the same prison and break his brother out. That is not systematic theology but perhaps a sermon illustration—and we should always remember that the proclamation of the work of Christ is to be precisely the "actual event" of atonement for those to whom the word comes. Such an illustration serves the purpose of fiducial influence because in the utter dereliction of Christ sinners see the end of their "wrong road" and in his resurrection we are given a vision of the goal that God desires for them. This is a dramatic way of saying that God truly "made him to be sin who knew no sin, so that in him we might become the righteousness of God" (2 Corinthians 5:21).

These images again call to mind the Christus Victor theme and the passages in the Old Testament that speak of God defeating the powers that threaten creation. But the picture is very different from that of the common superhero motif, typified by Marduk's slaying of Tiamat in the Babylonian creation epic. Instead of achieving victory by beating up all the evildoers, Jesus is the one who gets beaten up, and thereby is victorious and saves creation.

Ephesians 4:9-10, another passage that may lie behind the idea of a descent into hell, suggests another image that is expressed in an Advent hymn written by Ambrose of Milan.[212]

God the Father is his source,
Back to God he runs his course;
Down to death and hell descends,
God's high throne he reascends.

He leaves heaven to return;
Trav'ling where dull hellfires burn;
Riding out, returning home
As the Savior who has come.

The picture here is that of the "Grand Tour"[213]—the ruler taking possession of his domains as he travels through them. In the end, nothing is excluded. All creation is to be renewed, reconciled to God by the blood of Christ's cross.

CHAPTER VII

REGENERATION THROUGH WORD AND SPIRIT

The Need to Transpose Justification

The belief that people are justified in God's sight because of the life, death, and resurrection of Jesus Christ has been an important aspect of the Christian faith ever since Paul wrote his letters to the Galatians and the Romans. It became of particular—and divisive—importance in the sixteenth century when the reformers saw the doctrine of justification by grace through faith alone as a central aspect of Christian teaching. That position was set out in the confession presented by the Lutherans at the Diet of Augsburg in 1530.[214]

> Furthermore, it is taught that we cannot obtain forgiveness of sin and righteousness before God through our merit, work, or satisfactions, but that we receive forgiveness of sin and become righteous before God out of grace for Christ's sake through faith when we believe that Christ has suffered for us and that for his sake our sin is forgiven and righteousness and eternal life are given to us. For God will regard and reckon this faith as righteousness in his sight, as St. Paul says in Romans 3[:21-26] and 4[:5}.

The Roman Catholic response to the Confession agreed that we cannot merit salvation by our own powers alone, but rejected the claim that works play no role in justification, saying that "all Catholics confess that our works of themselves have no merit, but that God's grace makes them worthy of eternal life."[215] Much more recently The Lutheran World Federation and the Roman Catholic Church, later joined by the World Methodist Council, approved the Joint Declaration on the Doctrine of Justification which reached significant, though incomplete, agreement on historically debated issues in connection with justification.[216]

A full discussion of justification today would require consideration of this document as well as other matters. Recent study of Luther by Finnish theologians has suggested that his view of salvation actually had some similarity with that of the Orthodox tradition, while the "new perspective on Paul" in New Testament theology has challenged influential Augustinian-Lutheran-Calvinist interpretations of that apostle.[217] But for our purposes it is necessary to concentrate on challenging questions which in a way are even more fundamental. Must a legal concept like justification be the primary way in which we speak about salvation? Are the existential questions that people ask today about guilt and forgiveness like those that prompted the Reformation's teachings on justification, or should we now be addressing different concerns? To put it briefly, is the very concept of justification obsolete?[218]

These questions are not new. Over fifty years ago Paul Tillich said that the traditional doctrine of justification is "so strange to the modern man that there is scarcely any way of making it intelligible to him."[219] A statement from the 1963 Lutheran World Assembly in Helsinki, which was unable to come to a consensus on the doctrine of justification, expressed its dilemma in similar words.

> The man of today no longer asks, "How can I find a gracious God?" His question is more radical, more elementary: he asks about God as such, "Where is God?" He suffers not from God's wrath, but from the impression of his absence; not from sin but from the meaninglessness of his own existence; he asks not about a gracious God, but whether God really exists.[220]

People today may wonder about the relevance of Christian doctrines and question the reality of God for various reasons, but one of them is surely the rise and spread of scientific views of the world. Extreme views are expressed by some atheists to the effect that the successes of science have proved that there is no God and that religious language is essentially meaningless.[221] But even if such radical claims are not accepted (and in fact their attacks are directed against rather puerile understandings of God and religious faith), the particular language of justification, and especially the forensic understanding of it to be discussed below, does not easily make contact with people who are imbued with a scientific understanding of the world.

"Justification" and "forensic" are legal terms, and the metaphors for the forensic understanding are those of the "forum," the court. We are saved, as Barth put it, because of "the judge judged in our place."[222] The person who stands guilty before the judge is declared righteous by the judge because of the righteousness of that same judge. Such language is certainly biblical and is prominent in the theological tradition, and it has spoken deeply to many people though the centuries. But it does not speak well to a scientific world. The use of legal language does not contradict any scientific truth—the idea of "laws of nature" comes, after all, from the legal and religious realms.[223] But the laws that scientists speak of do not convict or acquit people.

I emphasized in Chapter I that my purpose is not to eliminate or declare invalid all non-scientific ways of speaking about salvation. I am not proposing that preachers and teaching theologians should never use judicial language or images, or that a new "scientific" understanding of justification must replace the judicial one in all situations. But we do need other ways of speaking that are legitimized by the Bible and the Christian tradition *and* that can make contact with the types of consonance between theology and science that recent dialogue between those disciplines has achieved in connection with the doctrine of creation.

What is called for then is not elimination of the judicial concept of justification but, in a sense, transformation of it. Einstein's relativity theory in physics provides a helpful analogy here. That theory allows us to describe phenomena in different reference frames by providing a way to transform observations in one frame to those in another. The measurements of time intervals or distances by two observers in relative motion will, in general, differ, but Einstein's theory makes it possible to see how both sets of observations can be in accord with the same fundamental law.[224] In a similar way, we need to be able to speak of the reality that the theological tradition has called justification from the standpoint of those who look at the world in terms of the natural sciences, so that people using a scientific frame of reference will in a basic sense be saying the same thing as those using a legal reference frame. The concepts which we employ must have scriptural legitimacy and also be able to facilitate communication with scientific understandings of the world.

It is not necessary, however, to find new "scientific" equivalents for every traditional term. Such an attempt would be likely to give us only clumsy circumlocutions. In particular, we should not try to replace the crucial word "faith" with some supposedly scientific equivalent. Of course psychology and the other human sciences can help us to understand the processes of human belief and commitment, but saving faith is not just a psychological concept. The use of words such as faith, sin, and righteousness in the following should be a reminder that our goal is not to eliminate or replace the traditional concept of justification but to restate it in a way that it can be more easily communicated to human beings in a scientific world.

We should also remember that "faith" is not something that is alien to the scientific enterprise, even though some people try to play off "faith" and "reason" as mutually exclusive. Unless a person had some confidence that phenomena in the world make some kind of sense, there would be no point in devoting one's efforts toward systematic study of the world. That confidence can be justified *a posteriori* for particular classes of phenomena by the success of the scientific approach, but the scientist approaching some new phenomenon cannot prove *a priori* that it will be possible to understand it in a satisfactory way.

The Doctrine of Regeneration

We have seen in the previous chapters that the idea of new creation as a reorientation of the temporal course of the world provides a way to make contact with science-theology dialogue. This work of new creation begins with what happens to human beings because of the life, death, and resurrection of Jesus of Nazareth. One way of speaking about what takes place is to say that they are "reborn" or "renewed."

Related terms such as "regeneration" and "renovation" have been used in discussions of salvation in traditional theology. In his later Apology for the Confession that had been presented at Augsburg, Melanchthon used "rebirth" and "regeneration" as concepts closely related to "justification." For example, we are told there that "[B]ecause 'to be justified' means that out of unrighteous people righteous people are made or regenerated, it also means that they are pronounced or regarded as righteous."[225] A bit later he says, "Therefore we are justified by faith alone, justification being understood as the making of a righteous person out of an unrighteous one or as regeneration."[226]

Nearly fifty years later the Formula of Concord recognized that usage and noted that "*regeneratio* (that is, 'rebirth')" had several senses.[227] Narrowly it could include just "forgiveness of sins and our adoption as children of God," but more broadly it could mean "sancti-fication or renewal." Regeneration could even "include both the forgiveness of sins because of Christ alone and the resultant renewal."[228] But the theological debates of the intervening half century had shown that it was important to avoid any ambiguity and to be completely clear that the righteousness of the new life of the believer was not to be seen alongside the righteousness of Christ as a cause of the believer's fundamental change of status. Thus the writers of the Formula ex-plicitly distinguished between justification and regeneration or renewal.[229] This was part of the development in the period of Protes-tant scholasticism of detailed analyses of an "order of salvation" (ordo salutis) that supposedly had to be gone through, one in which "re-generation" and "renovation" were stages.[230]

The crucial distinction that is traditionally made here is between justification and sanctification. Those who have been justified entirely by God's work are then able to cooperate with God in sanctification. Those two aspects of God's work must be kept separate logically so that the human work involved in sanctification is not seen as some-thing that merits, even in part, God's declaration that they are righteous. God, as Paul says, "justifies the ungodly" (Romans 4:5). We can use the term re-creation in place of regeneration to "include both the for-giveness of sins because of Christ alone and the resultant renewal"[231] if we remember two traditional aspects of the word "creation" itself. It can encompass God's act of bringing all things into being "from noth-ing" (creatio ex nihilo)—and thus without anything else having any causal role in the action—as well as God's ongoing preservation of creatures and activity with them (creatio continua).[232] Thus re-cre-ation can include both what the tradition has called justification and sanctification, God's initial act in which a sinner is declared righteous and God's ongoing work in the justified person's life. We do need to be aware constantly of whether re-creation is being used in its strict sense, in which it parallels the traditional term justification, or more loosely, to include what has usually been called sanctification.

The fact that justification can be spoken of alternatively as a work of re-creation is an obvious, but nevertheless important, parallel be-tween the central Christian message of salvation and Christian teaching about creation. It means that we can make use of ways in which science has been able to inform the doctrine of creation in order to illumine our understanding of God's work of salvation. And because of this first parallel we are encouraged to look for others.

The Work of Word and Spirit

The concept of forensic justification means that God, as judge, declares sinners righteous. More precisely, God *imputes* to them the righteousness of Christ. The powerful link between the biblical concept of creation by the divine Word (Genesis 1; Psalm 33:6; Isaiah 55:10-11; John 1:3; Hebrews 1:3) and forensic justification is therefore crucial for our argument. The term "forensic" calls up, as we have noted, images of courtrooms and legal proceedings, but the fundamental meaning of forensic justification is that sinners are righteous because God's Word says that they are. God's Word is creative precisely because it does what it says (Jeremiah 23:29). The work of regeneration, of giving new life to those who are spiritually dead, is a prime example of this creative power.

The fourth chapter of Romans clearly identifies the intimate connections between the divine works of creation, justification, new life, and eschatological hope. There we are told that the God who "justifies the ungodly" (4:5) is also the one "who gives life to the dead" and "calls into existence things that do not exist" (4:17). And because of this it is possible for us to be, like Abraham, "hoping against hope" (4:18). All of these works bear the same mark of the resurrection of the Crucified.[233]

The idea that God "imputes" or "reckons" the righteousness of Christ to sinners has sometimes been accused of making justification a legal fiction. The fact that in these "court proceedings" there are no "mitigating circumstances" in favor of the accused seems to strengthen the impression that God simply treats sinners "as if" they were righteous even though they are not. But what God says is never fictitious. The claim that imputation gives only a pretense of righteousness is like a notion that the "Let there be" commands of Genesis 1 created only the illusion of a world. But in reality God brought the real cosmos we inhabit into being through the *logos*. That Greek word can mean "reason" as well as "word," and the statement in the prologue of the Fourth Gospel that all things came into being through the *logos* has been seen by a number of writers as a link with scientific belief in the underlying rationality of the world.[234] God willed that there be a universe that makes sense. "He spoke, and it came to be; he commanded, and it stood firm" (Psalm 33:9).

And when God declares a sinner righteous, that person begins in reality to participate in the righteousness of Christ which is God's goal for creation.[235] This is not the traditional Roman Catholic concept of *infused* righteousness, in which sinners become righteous because divine grace is put into them.[236] Instead it is the very declaration of righteousness that brings about righteousness. We have to take with full seriousness Paul's statement—shocking as it is to conventional religion and morality—that God "justifies the ungodly." And by that very act God make them godly.

God creates a new relationship through the Word, but the Word of God does not work alone. We should always picture it as acting together with the Spirit, the two "hands of God" in Irenaeus' phrase.[237] In Genesis 1:2 the spirit of God moves over the primordial deep before God speaks, and in Psalm 33:6 "the word of the LORD" and "the breath of his mouth" are both ways of speaking about the creation of the heavens. The Spirit is seen as being involved especially with living things (Psalm 104:29-30), and in the Nicene Creed is described as "Lord and giver of life."

"So faith comes from what is heard, and what is heard comes through the word of Christ" (Romans 10:17). Atonement between God and humanity rests upon the actual event of the cross, the death and resurrection of Jesus outside Jerusalem under Pontius Pilate. But that event would have no effect on people today if it were not proclaimed. The equally actual event in which the cross and resurrection encounter people is the proclamation of the good news that Jesus "was handed over to death for our trespasses and was raised for our justification" (Romans 4:25). Ultimately all theological work should in some way support and encourage that proclamation.

Faith is the new relationship created by Word and Spirit. And the work of the Spirit in salvation is first of all to bring people to faith, for "No one can say 'Jesus is Lord' except by the Holy Spirit" (1 Corinthians 12:3). So the church prays that God would "accompany your Word with your Spirit and power."[238] The impossibility of confessing the lordship of Christ without the activity of the Holy Spirit indicates that in this part of the Spirit's work the human subject is passive. As Luther explained this work in the Small Catechism, "I believe that by my own understanding or strength I cannot believe in Jesus Christ my LORD or come to him, but instead the Holy Spirit has called me through the gospel, enlightened me with his gifts, made me holy and kept me in the true faith."[239] To put it another way, the new life that God creates does not exist prior to God's gift of faith.

Since this new creative work of God comes through hearing the Word, it might seem that it must always be something episodic and discontinuous. That would mean that there could not really be any constant progress in the Christian life. As Romans 4 indicates, the justification of the ungodly is a radically new act like creation of the universe out of nothing and the resurrection of the dead. We were "dead through our trespasses" and God "made us alive together with Christ" (Ephesians 2:5). Is the Christian then always in the same condition as in "the hour I first believed"?

Attention to the parallel with creation can keep us from that mistake. As we have already emphasized, God's work of creation includes not only the origination of the universe but also the ongoing preservation of creatures and cooperation with them in their activities. Scripture affirms in many places (e.g., Psalm 104:10-30; Psalm 145:15-16; Matthew 6:26-30) that God is continually working to provide for creatures. That is the aspect of creation that the catechisms of the Reformation emphasize in their explanations of the First Article of the creed.[240]

Traditional doctrines of providence have spoken not only of God's preservation of creatures and governance of them toward their intended ends, but also of "the co-operation of the divine power with all subordinate powers, according to the preestablished laws of their operation, causing them to act, and to act precisely as they do."[241] Older theologies understood cooperation (sometimes called, less felicitously, "concurrence") to be subordinate to preservation, but modern science points us in the other direction. Investigations ranging from the physics of elementary particles and the development of new biological species to the formation of stars and the expansion of the entire universe show that the world does not consist of inert pieces of matter but of dynamic entities whose basic properties depend on interactions with other entities. In view of this reality we ought to understand God's preservation of creatures to take place through the divine cooperation with their physical processes. It is by cooperating with creatures that God preserves them.[242]

This insight helps us better understand the work of re-creation. Having begun new life by joining sinners to the death and resurrection of Christ (Romans 6:1-11), God cooperates with and sustains that life. This work of preservation through repentance and forgiveness is always a return to the dying and rising of baptism, as Luther emphasizes in explaining the meaning of that sacrament for daily life.[243] But there is continuity—not between the old sinful self and the new, but in the life of the new self. One might try to draw parallels with quantum mechanics, in which there are aspects of both continuity and discontinuity.

The ongoing process of sanctification is now one in which the believer is able to cooperate to some degree with the Holy Spirit. Everything depends ultimately on God, but in this work of hallowing believers, just as in providing the necessities of life in the world for creatures, God acts through second causes.

The Instruments of New Creation

In the previous pages I have continued to distinguish between the beginning of new life in Christ which parallels the origination of the world and the sustenance and growth of that new life which is analogous to God's ongoing cooperation with, and preservation of, all creatures in the world. The human cooperates in the latter work but is entirely passive in the former. Babies do not cooperate in their own conception. The strong form of the doctrine of justification which insists that it—including the faith that receives God's gift—is entirely God's work means that there is no place for synergism, the idea that people cooperate in their own justification. Suggestion that human will and effort play some positive role in conversion was decisively rejected by both Calvin and the Formula of Concord.[244]

Reflection on the parallels between creation and new creation, however, should warn us not to overreact to the word "synergism" in discussions of salvation. It is, after all, the Greek-based equivalent of the Latin-based term "cooperation" that is used in connection with God's ongoing work of creation.

In bringing about new creation God does cooperate with creatures, although not with the human will. Instead God works with and through the "means of grace," Word and sacraments, in order to bring about and sustain the new life in Christ. God does not, in general, act immediately, but through those means. It is through the proclamation of the Word that Christ crucified is made a reality for people and creates faith (Romans 10:17; Galatians 3:1). This is true first of the word that is preached and its written form in the scriptures, but also of the "visible words" of baptism and the Lord's Supper.[245] This does not mean that we can explain how preaching, let alone the use of water or bread and wine, can bring about faith. (The difficulty is especially obvious with the baptism of infants, a difficulty which is lessened to some extent when we understand faith as essentially trust and not simply an intellectual act.)

God's activity in salvation through these instruments provides another parallel with the divine activity in creation, where God generally works through natural processes. But unlike God's normal use of human abilities to speak and write, or of water and food in nature, in which God limits divine cooperation to the natural capacities of those instruments, the Holy Spirit does something with words, water and bread and wine that is more than "natural" when they convey God's forgiveness and acceptance. In this sense the effects of spoken or printed words and the sacraments can be called "miraculous." These, however, are hidden miracles. While we may observe a change in a person's attitude, we cannot detect faith scientifically and thus do not observe any effects that exceed what our scientific understanding of nature would allow.

This should remind us that there are limits to the parallels that we can draw between God's work of creating life and God's actions in bringing people from spiritual death to life. Faith is an essential aspect of this work of regeneration (or in forensic language, of justification) but putting one's ultimate trust in the God revealed in Christ is not "natural" for those who are accustomed to the atmosphere of sin. The conversion of sinners itself could be called miraculous because God does it not only without their cooperation but also in spite of their resistance.[246] The fact that not all people who are exposed to the same proclamation of the Gospel are converted is another indication of this limitation. Attempts to explain this either by saying that God does not really want all to be saved (in spite of 1 Timothy 2:3) or that certain people cooperate in some degree with the Holy Spirit (in spite of Ephesians 2:8-9) are unsatisfactory. We have to admit that we simply don't know why some come to faith and others do not.

These limitations should not, however, obscure the fact that God's use of physical elements, and even of human technology,[247] in the sacraments provides a significant point of contact between the divine activity in creation and the renewal and reorientation of the creation. The same God who makes life in the world possible through water and food uses the same elements, but now in special ways, to create and sustain the new life of faith in Christ.

The New Humanity

The focus of many discussions of justification and sanctification on what takes place for an individual person who responds to the gospel has often resulted in neglect of the corporate aspect of salvation. However, the New Testament speaks of the result of God's saving work not simply as an assortment of regenerated individuals but as a new humanity, the Body of Christ. The role of the sacraments as the means of this renewal is notable.

"For in the one Spirit we were all baptized into one body" (1 Corinthians 12:13).

"The bread that we break, is it not a sharing in the body of Christ? Because there is one bread, we who are many are one body, for we all partake of the one bread" (1 Corinthians 10:16-17).

The biological image of the Body of Christ is significant. It suggests, as Paul discusses in some detail in 1 Corinthians 12, that individual persons are brought together to form a super-personal organism of which Christ is the head.

Billions of years ago single-celled organisms were the only form of life on earth. Symbiotic relationships eventually gave rise to multicellular organisms in one of the major transitions of evolutionary history. (The mitochondria in our cells, with their own DNA, are probably one result of this process.) The development of more complex life forms eventually made it possible for intelligence to emerge in a species. Teilhard de Chardin suggested that in an analogous way the Body of Christ should be seen as the next stage in evolution.[248] We should not, however, understand this as simply the next step in a more or less direct process of development. Bearing in mind the fact that God's work of new creation is a correction of the sinful course of history, we should see it rather as an aspect of the reorientation of the historical process by which humanity is turned back toward the end for which God intended it.

The formation of a corporate entity does not mean that individual personality is to be crushed out. On the contrary, as Paul's elaboration of the image in 1 Corinthians 12 brings out, being part of one body means that each member can be fully her or himself. As Teilhard put it, "Union creates . . . *differentiates* . . . [and] *personalizes*."[249]

The church is much more than the passive object of God's work of re-creation. It is also the "workshop" of the Holy Spirit.[250] In this new community the Spirit continually brings to birth, renews, and strengthens faith in Christ. Luther's explanation of how the Holy Spirit brings "me" to faith that was quoted earlier continues with an emphasis on the corporate aspect of the work: "just as he calls, gathers, enlightens, and makes holy the whole Christian church on earth and keeps it with Jesus Christ in the one common, true faith. Daily in this Christian church the Holy Spirit abundantly forgives all sins—mine and those of all believers."[251] Again God works with ordinary means— a community with all too many imperfections and one that can be studied with the tools of the human and social sciences—in order to reorient creation toward its intended goal.

CHAPTER VIII

COSMIC SALVATION

The Scope of Atonement

To this point we have dealt almost entirely with God's saving work as it relates to humanity. That is quite traditional, and in fact many Christians consider it rather strange if someone suggests that salvation extends beyond the human race. "God has not died for the white heron," the Second Musician says in Yeats' play, *Calvary*.[252]

In line with such thinking, the Christian understanding of creation also has had an almost exclusively anthropocentric focus. Even though this has not usually been made explicit, it has been thought that all the rest of creation is here simply for our use and enjoyment, and that only humanity has any real value in God's sight.[253] That means, among other things, that the "dominion" given to humanity in Genesis 1:28 can be treated as a license to exploit nature, with consequences that we can see in our modern environmental crisis. And if only humanity is of real importance for God, then it follows that only humanity will participate in the new creation. Everything else serves simply as a "launching pad," in Rahner's phrase, to start us off on our way to heaven.[254]

Some trends in twentieth century theology reinforced such views. Bultmann, for example, argued that while a person can confess God as the one to whom her or his existence is owed, "statements which speak of God's actions as cosmic events are illegitimate." Thus we cannot affirm God as creator of the world in general.[255] If this were the case there would be little reason for the church to be concerned with the natural world or for theology to take into account the sciences that study the world.

But the sciences themselves make it clear that who we are depends on our relationships with the rest of creation. We are "carbon based lifeforms"—that chemical element is essential for our bodies and their operations, as it is for all known living things. The nuclei of carbon atoms, as well as those of heavier elements, were formed in the cores of earlier generations of stars. They were spread through the galaxy by supernova explosions and eventually became part of our solar system and of the earth's biosphere. "We are" quite literally, "made of star stuff," as Carl Sagan said.[256] And through our evolutionary history we are organically related to all other terrestrial species, living and extinct. Today's environmental problems have brought us to realize that what happens to one species of an ecosystem affects all its other members. We are creatures who owe our existence first to the God who is the creator of the universe, and secondarily to other parts of that universe in and through which God acts.

Our discussion here, and especially that in Chapter IV, has shown that we are creatures of God who in our evolutionary history have sinned, straying from the path that God meant for us to walk. As sinners we are saved by the participation in that history of the Word of God who assumed our evolved flesh, who died in solidarity with the losers in the "struggle for life," and whose resurrection gives hope that the whole creation will be rescued from futility (Romans 8:18-25). Scripture is quite clear that God's saving and hallowing work extends beyond the human race. We have already noted the biblical texts that promise new heavens and a new earth, the passages in Ephesians and Colossians that speak of God's plan to unite "all things" in Christ and the reconciliation of all things through the cross, and the promise in Romans 8:18-25 that "the creation" will be liberated from bondage.

Some care is needed in pursuing this idea however. In the first place, the old idea that the sin of the first humans brought about some change in the physical nature of the whole world has to be rejected. There is abundant evidence that creatures were dying for billions of years before humanity came on the scene. Pathogens and predation have been around for a long time—the teeth of Tyrannosaurus rex were not those of a vegetarian! And the notion that the Second Law of Thermodynamics went into effect only when Eve bit into the apple is worth mentioning only as a joke.[257]

The consistency of results that are obtained when we explore the distant past with the assumption that the laws of physics in that epoch were the same as those today is remarkable. There was no "cosmic fall" in the sense of a radical change in the laws of physics when humans first sinned. The curse on the ground of Genesis 3:17-19, if the writer indeed thought that there had been no weeds and no need for hard work before sin, must be seen as further divine accommodation to an outdated understanding of earth history. But we can think of it in a way analogous to the understanding of death that was presented in Chapter IV. People separated from God see the difficulties involved in agriculture (and by extension other aspects of life in the world) differently than would those in a sinless condition.

This does not mean that sin has no effect outside humanity. The damage that we do to the rest of creation is the most obvious example. It is not only the immediate effects of our actions on nature (such as hunting species to extinction) but also the indirect results of our actions and our very existence that may make other species, if not "sinful," yet in some ways less than what God desires for them. And as we will see later in this chapter, if there are intelligent extra-terrestrials, then sin almost certainly has a genuinely cosmic scope.

In addition, we need to be circumspect in our discussion here because science can give us only modest assistance in understanding the renewal of creation. The current picture of a universe that apparently will expand at an ever-increasing rate forever seems to have no place for such a concept. This means that God must do something genuinely new, something not included in our presently understood laws of physics. However, God has revealed virtually nothing about the details of creation's final future. Responsible theology can therefore say very little about what salvation means beyond the bounds of our species and how that may be brought about. Some conjectures about these matters are legitimate, but we must appreciate that they *are* conjectures and realize that there is little point in going into great detail with what is at best intelligent guesswork.

For that reason the discussions of some rather large topics in this concluding chapter will be relatively brief.

Salvation Outside the Church?

It will be helpful to begin with a question that does pertain only to humans. Is it true—and if so, in what sense is it true—that, in the classic phrase of the third century bishop Cyprian, "There is no salvation out of the church" (*Quia salus extra ecclesiam non est*)?[258] If being outside the church means not being formally affiliated with the institutional church, then we have to say that the Bible never makes such a claim. It does say that salvation is through Christ, and if we understand the church as the Body of Christ then the claim is less problematic, though we then have to ask what kind of relationship with Christ is involved. Does it require explicit knowledge of Jesus? Can there be, as Rahner suggested, "anonymous Christians"?[259] Or is that like thinking that we can help poor people just by declaring them anonymously rich?[260]

While the New Testament does make exclusive claims about salvation through Christ (as in Acts 4:12), there are also verses that suggest that salvation still has a very wide range. After all, God "desires everyone to be saved and to come to the knowledge of the truth" (1 Timothy 2:4). The passages in Ephesians and Colossians that refer to the reconciliation with God of "all things" may be understood to mean all *kinds* of things and not all individuals of every species, but the impression that we get is of a salvation that is generous and wide-sweeping. Recall that in a passage we discussed earlier, Jesus said that when he was lifted up from the earth he would draw all—not some—people to himself (John 12:32). God is, if anything, looking for ways to get people in rather than to keep them out.

We have to admit that we simply are not sure whether salvation for humans is universal or not. We are never told in scripture of any particular person who will ultimately be lost. The New Testament (e.g., Mark 9:43-48) and the Christian tradition are clear that there is a condition of damnation that we call hell, but we cannot say with absolute certainty, as Teilhard de Chardin pointed out, that anyone will ultimately be in that condition.[261] With our natural desire to see evildoers destroyed (as in Psalm 104:35) we might bear in mind an anecdote about Abraham Lincoln. When someone questioned him about the fact that he showed no anger toward his enemies and told Lincoln that he should not try to befriend his enemies but destroy them, the president is supposed to have replied, "Do I not destroy my enemy by making him my friend?"[262]

We may hope that all will ultimately be saved, but we cannot say "with the certainty of faith" that they are. It is finally up to God. But we can ask, with due caution, how God *might* reconcile all people to himself through the cross of Christ—even those who have consciously rejected Christianity, even those who have never heard of Jesus Christ, even those who believe in no God of all. A few possibilities suggest themselves, none of them free of problems.

Perhaps God could simply save everybody regardless of their commitments, beliefs, or actions: "All have won and all shall have prizes."

But what kind of reconciliation would it be for Hitler, unrepentant to the end, to be brought into the heavenly city to mingle with those murdered in Auschwitz? What is the ultimate state of one finally closed in upon the self like a single ingrown toenail?

Christianity is of course not the only faith, but it is too simplistic to speak simply of "Christianity and other religions" as if all the latter could simply be grouped together. Christianity has a unique historical relationship with Judaism, one that has resulted in agreement on some basic beliefs but unfortunately also in conflict and persecution. It is possible—and in a paradoxical way more generous to Muslims than some other views of their religion—to consider Islam as a Christian heresy, as did John of Damascus, one of the first Christian theologians to encounter that religion.[263] There are also some commonalities of both history and content with other faiths.

How might God's saving work in Christ be effective through these faiths? Ethical principles common to a wide range of religious and philosophical traditions have often been noted; we might think of the examples that C.S. Lewis gathered to illustrate what he called "the Tao."[264] For our purposes it is more important to look for similar theological concepts and especially those that might provide an appropriate role for Christ in other religions.

Christians and Jews share the Hebrew scriptures, albeit in different contexts and often with different interpretations. An observant Jew who awaits the coming of the Messiah and the Kingdom of God may well be more faithful to God's covenant than some who bear the name Christian. (Robert Browning's poem, "Holy-Cross Day," should give Christians some sobering thoughts in this regard.)[265] The Qur'an is in profound agreement with Christianity in speaking of God as "most beneficent, most merciful." It also gives Jesus high honors, though the fact that it denies his death on the cross, as we noted in Chapter II, is not just a disagreement about one historical fact but evidence of a quite different outlook.

One of the tenets of Japanese Pure Land Buddhism resembles the concept of justification by faith, and the Christian process theologian John Cobb has suggested that those in this tradition might be able to identify Amida Buddha, in whose Vow they are to trust, with Christ.[266] And to gain the knowledge of the Runes, Odin says in the Elder Edda,

Nine whole nights on a wind-rocked tree,
Wounded with a spear,

I was offered to Odin, myself to myself,
On that tree of which no man knows.[267]

That is probably a late Norse borrowing from Christianity, but the fact that that polytheistic religion (one with a heroically grim eschatology) could to some degree assimilate the cross is interesting. So concepts in the Christian tradition and those in other faiths are not totally disjoint.

Finally, there is the idea expressed by the apologist Justin Martyr in the mid-second century:

> We have been taught that Christ is the first-born of God, and we have declared above that he is the Word of whom every race of men were partakers; and those who lived reasonably [• ••• •• ό•••;"with reason," or "the Word."] are Christians, even though they have been thought atheists; as, among the Greeks, Socrates and Heraclitus, and men like them; and among the barbarians, Abraham, and Ananias, and Azarias, and Misael, and Elias, and many others whose actions and names we now decline to recount, because we know it would be tedious.[268]

Justin is defending Christians here against the charge that they make all people who lived before the time of Jesus "irresponsible." Still, the same argument could be applied, with some modifications, to people who came after Jesus' earthly life.

The problem, however, is the same one we encounter with other suggestions: The cross and resurrection of Christ, and indeed the incarnation, play no role. The first part of the prologue of John's Gospel has to bear all the weight, and the fact that the Word was made flesh plays no role. The *Logos* is primarily a teacher, and his instruction could take place without his incarnation.[269] But perhaps there is some essential relationship between the way of living "with reason" and the way of the cross. Christ is, after all, spoken of in scripture not only as the Word but also as the Wisdom of God. In 1 Corinthians 1:18-31 Paul sets out the paradox of the "foolishness" of the cross as God's wisdom, and he speaks in verse 30 of Christ as "wisdom from God." And while it is based on a negative valuation of the body which Christianity cannot accept, Socrates' statement on the day of his death that "the true votary of philosophy . . . is always pursuing death and dying" may give us a hint of the cross.[270]

Salvation Beyond Humanity?

In view of the statements in the New Testament that we referenced earlier in this chapter, we have to take seriously questions about the place of non-human parts of creation in God's final future. The child's question, "Will my cat go to heaven?" should not be dismissed condescendingly, even though we know virtually nothing about what "cat heaven" might be. In fact, the question should not really be about other animals "going to heaven," because the biblical vision for humans is not so much one of "going to heaven" as of "the holy city, the new Jerusalem, coming down out of heaven from God" (Revelation 21:2). It is a picture of God's heavenly reality coming to a resurrected earth, a renewed creation. And if it is a renewed creation for humans, it must in some way include others creatures, parts of our environment without which we would not be what we are.

But we should not imagine that God cares only for humans, or that other living things will just be along for the eschatological ride. Isaiah's vision (11:1-9) of the peaceable kingdom should not be taken too literally. (Would lions would really be lions if they ate straw like oxen?) But the fact that it is expressed in terms of wolves, calves, and other animals should not be ignored.

How might the cross and resurrection of Christ be instrumental in bringing about the reconciliation of nature? The old soteriological axiom, "That which He [the Second Person of the Trinity] has not assumed He has not healed,"[271] made the point that Christ saves us in our full humanity by taking on that full humanity. And since our humanity is organically related to that of all other terrestrial species, living and dead, so is that of Christ. In assuming human flesh he took on our evolutionary history. This makes it possible to at least begin to think about how all earth's creatures might share in the reconciliation brought about by Christ.

This is not something that takes place without us, and it is not only a hope for a distant future. As people of renewed faith we are called afresh to the commission given to humanity in Genesis 2:15 and 1:26-28. We are to "serve" and "guard" the terrestrial garden and to exercise responsible dominion over it.[272] That dominion is part of our task of representing in the world the God who came not to be served but to serve (Mark 10:45). As the church helps to make people aware of the need to care for creation, the damage done to the world by sinful uses of technology can begin to be healed.

The work of creation's renewal is God's, but it is also a work in which God calls us to be intelligent participants and instruments. When the gifts of the gathered Christian community are brought forward for the celebration of the Lord's Supper, one suggested offertory prayer expresses this conviction that we are to be participants in God's work of the reorientation of creation.

> Blessed are you, O Lord our God, maker of all things. Through your goodness you have blessed us with these gifts. With them we offer ourselves to your service and dedicate our lives to the care and redemption of all that you have made, for the sake of him who gave himself for us, Jesus Christ our Lord. Amen.[273]

There is some similarity here with the Jewish concept of *tikkun olam*, "the mandate to be an active partner in the world's repair and perfection."[274] Today sciences such as ecology and climatology and science-based technologies are components of this partnership.

Salvation Beyond the Earth?

We return finally to a challenge that we heard in our opening chapter. Emerson, we recall, gave it as his opinion that it was "the irresistible effect of the Copernican astronomy to have made the theological *scheme of Redemption* absolutely incredible."

What he had in mind was not, strictly speaking, the "Copernican astronomy"—the heliocentric view of our planetary system. It was rather the concept of a "plurality of worlds" for which the Copernican theory opened the way and which had become widely accepted by Emerson's time. This was the idea that many of the stars were suns that had their own systems of planets which might harbor intelligent life. If that were the case, then it seemed to some people that any cosmic theological significance of events on earth, including the career of Jesus, had to be ruled out.[275]

These conclusions were not accepted by everyone. A book published twenty-two years after Emerson's statement by the Scottish physicist Sir David Brewster, *More Worlds Than One: The Creed of the Philosopher and the Hope of the Christian*, held that Christians should *expect* a plurality of worlds.[276] What could be the purpose of those suns, Brewster argued, if not to provide light and heat in order to make life possible on planets? The idea that we can so easily infer God's purpose from the arrangement of things in the universe, an idea shared by others of Brewster's time (he was writing a few years before Darwin's *Origin*) seems naïve to us today.

We now have much better astronomical information than Emerson and Brewster had, but we are still uncertain about the existence of extraterrestrial life. We do have an equation, that of Drake, for the number of advanced technical civilizations in our galaxy at present. The Drake equation gives that number as a product of six factors: the rate of star formation in the galaxy, the fraction of stars with planets, the number of planets suitable for life in each system, the probability of development of life under suitable conditions, the fraction of planets with life on which intelligence develops, the fraction of planets with intelligence on which advanced technical civilizations develop, and the lifetime of such a civilization. [277]

Drake's equation itself—in distinction from attempts to apply it—is not particularly controversial. If we believe that God acts through natural processes to bring forth life, then it is almost a tautology. But simply having a formula doesn't give us an answer. We need to know the numbers to put into the right side to get a number on the left side.

Astrophysics gives good estimates of the rate of star formation, and during the past twenty years astronomers have been finding more and more stars that have dark companions with masses on the scale of large planets.[278] Detection techniques have become refined enough to make it possible to pick out some planets with masses not too far from that of the earth, and we cannot rule out the possibility of life developing even in the atmosphere of a gas giant like Jupiter.

But from this point on our estimates become very vague. We don't know the probability of life evolving in the conditions of the early earth or in more exotic conditions. It seems to have taken about a billion years after the earth's crust cooled for life to begin, but at present we have a very small statistical sample—one!—of planets where we know for sure that this has happened. We know even less—in fact, almost nothing—about the probability of intelligence developing within a biosphere or of intelligent life developing a technical civilization. And we have little idea of how long such a civilization might, on average, last. That is especially so since we realize that we might destroy our own civilization by nuclear war or continued environmental irresponsibility.

So we don't know how many advanced technical civilizations may exist in our galaxy. There is little value in even "conservative" estimates if we don't know whether the values we use for the last three factors in the Drake equation are indeed conservative or overly generous. We would have to say something similar about just the number of intelligent extraterrestrial species, regardless of their technological levels.

When this equation was first proposed in 1961, it was generally assumed that an advanced technical civilization would be one that had developed radio and television so that we might expect to pick up its broadcast transmissions. Our own digital revolution in communications and use of satellite transmissions (aimed at Earth, with little of the energy going into space) has made us realize that the period during which an advanced technical civilization could be detected by picking up its electromagnetic signals might be rather short. This would not be the case if such a civilization were trying to advertise its existence, but many intelligent species might be too wary to do that.[279]

And there is another argument. In a discussion of the possibility of extraterrestrials, the physicist Enrico Fermi asked the simple question, "Where are they?"[280] Interstellar travel may be very difficult, but why have we picked up no electromagnetic transmissions from advanced technical civilizations if they exist? The fact that no such signals have been detected in spite of the effort devoted to searches for them suggests that the number of such civilizations is fairly small.

Having said that, it is certainly possible that there are intelligent extraterrestrials. But, before considering the theological implications of their existence, we should ask why they should automatically render "the theological *scheme of Redemption* absolutely incredible." We can get a clue by considering another statement by an American of a generation before Emerson, John Adams. In a letter to Thomas Jefferson, Adams advised that European professors not be hired for the University of Virginia. "They all believe," he wrote, "that great Principle which has produced this boundless universe, Newton's universe and Herschell's [*sic*] universe, came down to this little ball, to be spit upon by Jews. And until this awful blasphemy is got rid of, there never will be any liberal science in the world."[281]

This is a textbook example of a theology of glory. It is supposedly "blasphemy" to think that God might condescend to the limited conditions of a creature and suffer abuse. There are real theological questions raised by the possibility of extraterrestrials, but we should be aware that the kind of bad fundamental theology represented by Adams' letter may lurk behind many of the arguments against Christianity that claim to be based on a plurality of inhabited worlds.

The existence of extraterrestrials presents no difficulties for the Christian doctrine of creation, for there is no theological reason to think that God could not have created other intelligent species in the universe. The challenge comes from Christian beliefs about salvation and the idea that "all things" are reconciled to God by the cross and resurrection of Jesus of Nazareth on our planet some two thousand years ago. How could that person and those events be salvific for creatures thousands or millions of light years away and perhaps millions of years in the past?

If there are indeed intelligent extraterrestrials, we can be fairly certain that they have sinned. What we have inferred from our knowledge of evolution, that sin for humanity was inevitable though not necessary, applies to any other evolved intelligent species. If they, like us, have sinned and taken the wrong historical path, and if God's purpose is indeed to reconcile "all things" with Godself, then those creatures are in need of atonement. We cannot satisfactorily solve the problem of how the work of Christ might be effective beyond the earth by saying that extraterrestrials may not have fallen.[282]

How then might we understand their salvation?[283] Could the claim that Jesus Christ is the universal savior still make sense? As some have suggested with regard to the variety of terrestrial religions, we could just drop those universal claims for Jesus. Perhaps he is the savior only of terrestrial beings. But even if we ignore the theological problems with such an approach, it seems like an intellectually lazy way out. We ought at least to consider possibilities that retain a central role for what God has done on earth.

What about multiple incarnations? It may be possible to express that idea in a theologically coherent way. But as C. S. Lewis said, the image of species waiting in line for their turn is unattractive. He argued that if other species have sinned, God would achieve their redemption in other ways, and that those ways would have to be seen along with the incarnation on earth as part of the total drama of salvation.[284]

We have already considered the appeal of Justin Martyr to the pre-incarnate Christ, the *logos asarkos*, to deal with a similar question about the salvation of those on earth who had lived before Jesus' birth. It would be a straightforward matter to use the same type of argument in relation to extraterrestrials. But as we already saw, it is hard to do this if we want to retain an emphasis on the incarnation of the Word and the theology of the cross. On the other hand, Luther's argument for the omnipresence not only of the divine nature but also of Christ's humanity might be worth considering in this connection.[285]

Or Christ may be made present to the inhabitants of other planets in the same way that this has been happening for people on earth since the church was given the commission to "make disciples of all nations"—through the proclamation of Christ. In fact, religious radio and television messages that have been expanding outward from the earth at the speed of light for over sixty years may already have been picked up by some other intelligent species. The use of radio in this connection was already suggested by the cosmologist E. A. Milne in 1950.[286]

If there are intelligent extraterrestrials, Ephesians 3:9-10 suggests that the church is called to a cosmic mission. There we are told that part of God's plan is "that through the church the wisdom of God in its rich variety might be made known to the rulers and authorities in the heavenly places." The author of Ephesians did not have in mind inhabitants of other planets as we understand them today but angelic beings—"principalities and powers" in the older King James Version. Nevertheless, this verse does indicate that the message of reconciliation is to be proclaimed to all creatures, however we may understand them. When suitably demythologized, it might be understood to authorize a universal mission. Such a mission, however, will have to be freed from cultural, political, and economic imperialisms that too often have accompanied Christian missionaries on earth.

The Goal

The new relationship brought about by Christ is eschatological, one proper to God's final future.[287] God's atoning work has in view the goal of all creation—the Great Sabbath, the reign of God, the uniting of all things in Christ. That is the final future that God intends for creation, and in the Christ event that future has broken into the middle of the present world's history.

With our belief that God normally works in the world through natural processes, we have to ask how a genuine renewal of the universe that science observes could be brought about. Observations of the recession of galaxies and the microwave background radiation left over from the early universe indicate that the expansion of the universe is accelerating and will not be reversed. This is apparently driven by a still somewhat mysterious dark energy. Over billions of years, stars (including our own sun) and whole galaxies will burn out and collapse into massive black holes which will slowly decay. The average temperature of the universe will drop inexorably toward absolute zero. While it is possible that some suitably designed computers might continue to operate under these conditions, it is hard to see how anything resembling new creation might come into being.[288]

Since what we are concerned with is the renewal of the present creation, the new must be in some sense a creation from the old— creation *ex vetere*, as Polkinghorne puts it.[289] But it will indeed be new. Here Ted Peters' theology of prolepsis and his thesis that "God creates from the future, not the past" makes it possible to understand how something truly novel can come about.[290] Physicists today have not observed retrocausal effects, proceeding from the future into the past, but some solutions of Einstein's gravitational field equations, the advanced potentials of electromagnetic theory, and the properties of some models of dark energy provide theoretical possibilities for such phenomena.[291]

In particular, Robert John Russell has suggested that the resurrection of Jesus should be seen as "the first instantiation of a new law of nature."[292] It was something that had never been observed before, although it was not in conflict with the fundamental pattern of creation. The Christian hope is that that event will not be the only instance of that phenomenon, for Christ is proclaimed as "the first fruits of those who have fallen asleep" (1 Corinthians 15:20 RSV).

One important eschatological symbol is the Tree of Life. Mentioned briefly at the beginning of the Bible, it reappears at the very end. In Revelation 22:2 the Tree of Life is found not in a garden but in the middle of a city in which "death will be no more" (Revelation 21:4). Immortality is not something that humanity once had and forfeited but an eschatological hope. Yet the Tree of Life is an historical object that reverses conventional expectations about immortality, the cross of Christ.[293]

By reorienting human history, the work of Christ that is centered on the cross-resurrection event leads us again toward the goal that God intends for creation. Human rebellion against, and alienation from, God, sin that extends back to the beginning of humanity, meant that we were on the wrong road, moving away from that goal. We are now back on track. Led by the Spirit, we are, as the old gospel song puts it, "bound for the promised land." It is not just that "the sinner" is a new creation. She or he is part of God's new humanity. And our awareness of the corporate character of this new creation invites us to think about the even broader scope of this work of re-creation, the renewal of "all things."

ENDNOTES

1 Luther A. Weigle, ed., *The New Testament Octapla* (New York: Thomas Nelson and Sons, 1962), 1016.

2 *The Oxford English Dictionary, s.v.* "atone" and "atonement."

3 Gerhard O. Forde, "The Work of Christ" in Carl E. Braaten and Robert W. Jenson, eds., Christian Dogmatics, Vol. 2 (Philadelphia: Fortress Press, 1984), 5-99.

4 An older history is L. W. Grensted, *A Short History of the Doctrine of the Atonement* (Manchester: Manchester University, 1962; reprint of the 1920 edition). Peter Schmiechen, *Saving Power: Theories of Atonement and Forms of the Church* (Grand Rapids: Wm. B. Eerdmans Publishing Co., 2005) is an up-to-date study with detailed discussion of eight types. The survey in Forde, "The Work of Christ," is also helpful.

5 Stephan Finlan, Problems with Atonement (Collegeville, Minnesota: Liturgical Press, 2005), 5-38 and 42-44.

6 Anselm of Canterbury, "Why God Became Man" in Eugene R. Fairweather, ed., *A Scholastic Miscellany: Anselm to Ockham* (New York: Macmillan, 1970), 100-183.

7 Peter Abelard, "Exposition of the Epistle to the Romans (An Excerpt from the Second Book)" in Fairweather, *A Scholastic Miscellany*, 276-287.

8 Gustaf Aulén, *Christus Victor: An Historical Study of the Three Main Types of the Idea of the Atonement* (New York: Macmillan, 1961).

9 Schmiechen, *Saving Power*, and James Beilby and Paul R. Eddy, ed., with contributions by Gregory A. Boyd, Joel B. Green, Bruce R. Reichenbach, and Thomas R. Schreiner, *The Nature of the Atonement* (Downers Grove, Illinois: IVP Academic, 2006) are recent examples.

10 J. I. Packer and Mark Dever, *In My Place Condemned He Stood: Celebrating the Glory of the Atonement* (Wheaton, Illinois: Crossway, 2007) contains essays arguing for the necessity of penal substitution as well as useful bibliographic material.

11 See Packer and Dever, *In My Place Condemned He Stood*, 18-19, for this terminology and a brief criticism of such views.

12 Two books that embody many of these criticisms are Rita Nakashima Brock and Rebecca Ann Parker, Proverbs of Ashes: Violence, Redemptive Suffering and the Search for What Saves Us (Boston: Beacon, 2001), and Stephen J. Patterson, *Beyond the Passion: Rethinking the Death and Life of Jesus* (Minneapolis: Fortress Press, 2004).

13 J. Denny Weaver, *The Nonviolent Atonement* (Grand Rapids: Wm. B. Eerdmans Publishing Co., 2001).

14 Shailer Matthews, *The Atonement and the Social Process* (New York: Macmillan, 1930).

[15] Paul Tillich, *The Courage To Be* (New Haven: Yale University Press, 1952), 40-63.

[16] Steven Weinberg, *The First Three Minutes* (New York: Basic, 1977), 144.

[17] John M. Mangum, ed., *The New Faith-Science Debate: Probing Cosmology, Technology, and Theology* (Minneapolis: Fortress Press, 1989), vi.

[18] This is not to say that implications of evolution for soteriology have not been addressed at all. An early work is Rev. W. L. Walker, *The Cross and the Kingdom: As Viewed by Christ Himself and in the Light of Evolution* (Edinburgh: T. & T. Clark, 1902). "Christology Evolutionary Perspective" at http://www.counterbalance.org/rjr/bchri-body.html is a survey of some important later work. Two recent contributions are F. LeRon Shults, *Christology and Science* (Grand Rapids: Wm. B. Eerdmans Publishing Co., 2008); and the article by Celia Deane-Drummond, "Shadow Sophia in Christological Perspective: The Evolution of Sin and the Redemption of Nature," in *Theology and Science* 6 (2008): 13, with responses by James W. Haag, Nathan J. Hallanger, William O'Neill, S.J., and Robert John Russell.

[19] Quoted in Michael J. Crowe, *The Extraterrestrial Life Debate, 1750-1900* (Mineola, New York: Dover, 1999), 236. For further examples of this and other views on the religious implications of a plurality of worlds see the Subject Index entries under "Redemption and incarnation, Christian doctrines of" on page 678.

[20] John Shelby Spong, "Bishop Spong Q and A," Bishop Spong Q&A on the Origin of Good Friday, qna@johnshelbyspong.com, August 15, 2007. This and the following reference can be found in the archives at www.johnshelbyspong.com for the appropriate dates.

[21] This variety of anti-redemptionism may also make use of claims about the abusive character of traditional understandings of atonement, as in "Bishop Spong Q and A," Bishop Spong Q&A on the Danger of Atonement Theology, qna@johnshelbyspong.com, February 15, 2006. For another example see Gary Pence, "Sin: An Abusive Doctrine" in *dialog* 38 (1999): 294.

[22] Such attempts are not unknown today. See, e.g., the overstated claim of Frank J. Tipler, *The Physics of Immortality* (New York: Doubleday, 1994), 339: "Religion is now part of science."

[23] Siegbert H. Becker, *The Foolishness of God* (Milwaukee: Northwestern, 1982), 196-198.

[24] St. Athanasius, "On the Incarnation of the Word" in NPNF 2, IV, 36; George L. Murphy, "Chiasmic Cosmology and Atonement" in *Perspectives on Science and Christian Faith* 60 (2008): 214.

[25] Forde, "The Work of Christ."

[26] The fullest presentation of this program is George L. Murphy, *The Cosmos in the Light of the Cross* (Harrisburg, Pennsylvania: Trinity Press International, 2003). An earlier sketch is George L. Murphy, "Chiasmic Cosmology: An Approach to the Science-Theology Dialogue" in *Trinity Seminary Review* 13 (1991): 83.

[27] Justin Martyr, "The First Apology of Justin" in ANF I, 183. Plato's description in "Timaeus" is in *Collected Dialogues of Plato*, ed. Edith Hamilton and Huntington Cairns (Princeton: Princeton University Press, 1961), 1166.

[28] *Crux probat omnia*. Martin Luther, *D. Martin Luthers Werke, Kritische Gesammtausgabe, Band 5,* (Hermann Böhlau, 1892), 179, 31.

[29] Paul J. Achtemeier, *Mark* (Philadelphia: Fortress Press, 1975), 82, attributes the phrase to Martin Kähler.

[30] See, e.g., Sura IV of the Qur'an, vv. 157-158 in *The Holy Qur'an*, 3rd ed., with Arabic text and English translation and commentary by Abdullah Yusuf Ali (Damascus: XXXD´r Al-Mushaf, 1938), 230.

[31] Martin Luther, "Heidelberg Disputation, 1518" in Luther's Works (Philadelphia: Fortress pRESS, 1957), 39-70. Important discussions include Walter von Loewenich, *Luther's Theology of the Cross* (Minneapolis: Augsburg Publishing House, 1976) (a translation of the fifth German edition); Alister E. McGrath, *Luther's Theology of the Cross* (Cambridge, Massachusetts: Basil Blackwell, 1985); Gerhard O. Forde, *On Being a Theologian of the Cross: Reflections on Luther's Heidelberg Disputation, 1518* (Grand Rapids: Wm. B. Eerdmans Publishing Co., 1997; and Deanna A. Thompson, *Crossing the Divide: Luther, Feminism and the Cross* (Minneapolis: Fortress Press, 2004).

[32] Note, e.g., the title of Forde, *On Being a Theologian of the Cross.*

[33] This definition of theology is from J. A. Quenstedt, *The Nature and Character of Theology* (St. Louis: Concordia, 1986), 15, an abridged and edited translation by Luther Poellot of the first chapters of the 1696 edition of Quenstedt's *Theologia Didactico-Polemica sive Systema Theologicum.*

[34] Luther, "Heidelberg Disputation," 40.

[35] Luther's theses are quoted from Forde, *On Being a Theologian of the Cross*, because of the inclusive language of the translation there.

[36] Martin Hengel, *Crucifixion* (Philadelphia: Fortress Press, 1977), xi.

[37] Gregory Thaumaturgus, "To Theopompus, on the Impassibility and Passibility of God" in Volume 98 of *The Fathers of the Church* (Washington: The Catholic University of America, 1998), 152-173. For the issue in the early church generally see Joseph M. Hallam, *The Descent of God: Divine Suffering in History and Theology* (Minneapolis: Fortress Press, 1991).

[38] Martin Luther, "On the Councils and the Church," *Luther's Works*, Vol. 41 (Philadelphia: Fortress Press, 1966), 104.

[39] Martin Luther, "On the Councils and the Church."

[40] Marc Lienhard, *Luther: Witness to Jesus Christ* (Minneapolis: Augsburg Publishing House, 1982), 171.

[41] Kazoh Kitamori, *Theology of the Pain of God* (Richmond, Virginia: John Knox Press, 1965), a translation of the 5th Japanese edition. Jürgen Moltmann, *The Crucified God* (New York: Harper & Row, 1974). Eberhard Jüngel, *God as the Mystery of the World* (Grand Rapids: Wm. B. Eerdmans Publishing Co., 1983).

[42] Jüngel, *God as the Mystery of the World*, 13.

[43] http://www.orthodox.net/pascha/paschal-troparion-dblsided-4perside.pdf.

[44] Moltmann, *The Crucified God*, 207.

[45] Blaise Pascal, *The Pensées* (Baltimore: Penguin, 1961), #734, 252-253.

[46] Charles B. Cousar, *A Theology of the Cross: The Death of Jesus in the Pauline Letters* (Minneapolis: Fortress Press, 1990).

[47] This quotation from Irenaeus' *On the Apostolic Preaching* was quoted in this form by P. Evdokimov in *Scottish Journal of Theology* 18.1 (1965): 5.

[48] E.g., Christopher C. Knight, *Wrestling with the Divine: Religion, Science, and Revelation* (Minneapolis: Fortress Press, 2001), especially 108-109.

[49] Luther, "Heidelberg Disputation," 53.

[50] Forde, *On Being a Theologian of the Cross*, 72.

[51] The Latin text of the Heidelberg Theses is in *D. Martin Luthers Werke, Kritische Gesammtausgabe* (Weimar: Hermann Böhlau, 1883), Band 1, 353-374.

[52] George L. Murphy, *The Cosmos in the Light of the Cross* (Harrisburg, Pennsylvania: Trinity Press International, 2003), 28-34.

[53] Gordon D. Fee, *Paul's Letter to the Philippians* (Grand Rapids: Wm. B. Eerdmans Publishing Co., 1995), 196.

[54] Thomas F. Torrance, *Reality and Scientific Theology* (Edinburgh: Scottish Academic Press, 1985). See also Murphy, *The Cosmos in the Light of the Cross*, Chapter 2.

[55] Blaise Pascal, *Pensées/The Provincial Letters,* Eighteenth Letter (New York: Random House, 1941), 613.

[56] The Hebrew word translated "firmament" or "dome," *raqia*, has connotations of solidity. (Related words are used in connection with metal plates.) For discussion of this and the "waters above the heavens" see Denis O. Lamoureux, *Evolutionary Creation: A Christian Approach to Evolution* (Eugene, Oregon: Wipf and Stock, 2008), 120-125.

[57] Bruce Vawter, *The Inspiration of Scripture* (Philadelphia: Westminster, 1972) is a helpful introduction.

[58] Vawter, *The Inspiration of Scripture*, 40-42; Ford Lewis Battles, "God was Accomodating Himself to Human Capacity" in *Interpretation* 31 (1977): 19-38; Paul H. Seely, "The Date of the Tower of Babel and Some Theological Implications," *Westminster Theological Journal* 63 (2001): 15, especially section VIII.

[59] A recent discussion is Peter Enns, *Inspiration and Incarnation: Evangelicals and the Problem of the Old Testament* (Grand Rapids: Baker Academic, 2005).

[60] George L. Murphy, "Kenosis and the Biblical Picture of the World" in *Perspectives on Science and Christian Faith* 64 (2012): 157-165.

[61] G. R. Evans, *Sensus Plenior* in Alan Richardson and John Bowden, ed., *The Westminster Dictionary of Christian Theology* (Philadelphia: Westminster, 1983).

[62] Murphy, *The Cosmos in the Light of the Cross*, Chapter 6; John Polkinghorne, ed., *The Work of Love: Creation As Kenosis* (Grand Rapids: Wm. B. Eerdmans Publishing Co., 2001).

[63] E.g., Colin E. Gunton, *Christ and Creation* (Grand Rapids: Grand Rapids: Wm. B. Eerdmans Publishing Co., 1992), 85-86.

[64] Fee, *Paul's Letter to the Philippians*, 196.

[65] Murphy, *The Cosmos in the Light of the Cross*, Chapter 8.

[66] The phrase *etsi deus non daretur* was due originally to Grotius. The letter in which Bonhoeffer uses it is in Dietrich Bonhoeffer, *Letters and Papers from Prison*, enlarged edition (New York: Macmillan, 1972), 360-361.

[67] C. A. Coulson, *Science and Christian Belief* (London: Fontana, 1958), 41.

[68] George L. Murphy, "Divine Action and Divine Purpose" in *Currents in Theology and Mission* 36 (2009): 32.

[69] Karl Barth, *Dogmatics in Outline* (New York: Harper & Row, 1959), 58.

[70] George L. Murphy, *The Cosmos in the Light of the Cross* (Harrisburg, Pennsylvania: Trinity Press International, 2003), 169.

[71] Quoted in Arthur S. Peake, *Christianity: Its Nature and Truth* (London: Duckworth, 1908), 116.

[72] A. G. Hebert, *The Throne of David* (London: Faber and Faber, 1941), Chapter VI.

[73] *Lutheran Book of Worship* (Minneapolis: Augsburg Publishing House, 1978), 203.

[74] *The Interpreter's Dictionary of the Bible* (Nashville: Abingdon Press, 1962), s.v. "Adam," by B. S Childs. The word may be a proper name in 2:20, 3:17, 3:21 and 4:1. NRSV reads "the man" in all those places with "Adam" in the margin for the first three, while NIV reads "the man" in the first instance and "Adam" in the others.

[75] In the latter case Adam may be a place name, as in Joshua 3:16. Cf. Hans Walter Wolff, *Hosea* (Philadelphia: Fortress Press, 1974), 105, 121.

[76] Cf. Claus Westermann, *Genesis 1-11: A Commentary* (Minneapolis: Augsburg Publishing House, 1984), 276.

[77] *The Summa Theologica of Saint Thomas Aquinas*, Third Part, Q. I. Art. 3, Vol. II (Chicago: Encyclopedia Brittanica, 1952), 704 and references there.

[78] St. Augustine, "The City of God," Book XI, Chapter 6 in NPNF1, II, 208.

[79] A good overview is Ernst Mayr, *What Evolution Is* (New York: Basic, 2001). A collection of essays on cosmology and evolution which places them in historical and theological context is Keith B. Miller, ed., *Perspectives on an Evolving Creation* (Grand Rapids: Grand Rapids: Wm. B. Eerdmans Publishing Co., 2003).

[80] Charles Darwin, *On the Origin of Species by Natural Selection; or, the Preservation of Favored Races in the Struggle for Life* (London: J. W. Dent & Sons, 1972). This touched very briefly on human evolution, which Darwin dealt with more fully in *The Descent of Man and Selection in Relation to Sex*, revised ed. (Detroit: Gale Research, 1974). Wallace's contribution is described in H. Lewis McKinney, *Wallace and Natural Selection* (New Haven, Conneticuit: Yale University Press, 1972).

[81] Dennis R. Venema, "Genesis and the Genome: Genomics Evidence for Human-Ape Common Ancestry and Ancestral Hominid Population Sizes" in *Perspectives on Science and Christian Faith* 62 (2010): 166-178. *Nature* 420 (2002) contains a collection of papers on the mouse genome.

[82] Amir Aczel, *The Jesuit and the Skull: Teilhard de Chardin, Evolution, and the Search for Peking Man* (Riverhead, New York: Riverhead, 2007).

[83] See, e.g., Camilo J. Cela-Conde and Francisco J. Ayala, *Human Evolution: Trails from the Past* (New York: Oxford University Press, 2007).

[84] The Hebrew word used in Psalm 8:4 is actually '^{e}nosh, a less common term for the human than 'adham. The Septuagint translates it here with the same Greek word used to render 'adham in the Genesis creation accounts, *anthropos*.

[85] Some writers have adopted the Martian word *hnau* for intelligent creatures like humans and the fictional Martians from C. S. Lewis' science fiction novel, *Out of the Silent Planet* (New York: Macmillan, 1965).

[86] Simon Conway Morris, *Life's Solution: Inevitable Humans in a Lonely World* (New York: Cambridge, 2003), especially Chapter 9, "The non-prevalence of humanoids?"

[87] *Ibid.*, 271.

88 Eucharistic Prayer C of Holy Eucharist II, *The Book of Common Prayer* (New York: Church Publishing, 1979), 370.

89 E.g., Dennis Venema and Darrel Falk, "Does Genetics Point to a Single Primal Couple?" http://biologos.org/blog/does-genetics-point-to-a-single-primal-couple#.

90 David Wilcox, "Finding Adam: The Genetics of Human Origins," Chapter 11 in Miller, *Perspectives on an Evolving Creation*, 250-252.

91 Edward B. Davis, "The Word and the Works: Concordism and American Evangelicals" in Miller, *Perspectives on an Evolving Creation*, 43. For rejection of "death before the fall" see, e.g., http://www.answersingenesis.org/articles/2010/03/02/satan-the-fall-good-evil-could-death-exist-before-sin .

92 Peter C. Bouteneff, *Beginnings: Ancient Christian Readings of the Biblical Creation Narratives* (Grand Rapids: Baker Academic, 2008), 6, cites Justin Martyr and Irenaeus as well as the Book of Jubilees.

93 St. Athanasius, "On the Incarnation of the Word" in NPNF 2, IV, 38. The discussion on p.ixxi of the volume's Prolegomena by Archibald Robertson is also of interest.

94 Martin Luther, "Lectures on Genesis Chapters 1-5" in *Luther's Works*, Vol. 1 (St. Louis: Concordia Publishing House, 1958), 130.

95 James Barr, *The Garden of Eden and the Hope of Immortality* (Minneapolis: Fortress Press, 1992).

96 This is the phrase used by Darwin in *On the Origin of Species by Natural Selection* for what came to be called "evolution." In fact a form of the latter word—evolved—occurs only as the last word of the book.

97 Sarah Coakley, "Evolution and Sacrifice," *Christian Century* 126.21 (2009): 10.

98 See, e.g., Richard Leakey and Roger Lewin, *Origins Reconsidered: In Search of What Makes Us Human,* Chapter 16 (New York: Doubleday, 1992) and Carl Sagan and Ann Druyan, *Shadows of Forgotten Ancestors,* Chapters 14 and 15 (New York: Random House, 1992).

99 Philip Hefner, *The Human Factor: Evolution, Culture, and Religion* (Minneapolis: Fortress Press, 1993), especially 28-31. He attributes the idea to Ralph Wendell Burhoe.

100 For Lamarck's theory see Richard W. Burkhardt, Jr., *The Spirit of System: Lamarck and Evolutionary Biology* (Cambridge, Massachusetts: Harvard University Press, 1977), especially Chapter 6.

101 Mayr, *What Evolution Is*, 259.

102 Hefner, *The Human Factor*, 248.

103 Edward Gibbon, T*he Decline and Fall of the Roman Empire,* Volume I (Random House, New York), 69.

104 Barbara J. King, *Evolving God: A Provocative View on the Origins of Religion* (New York: Doubleday, 2007). Chapters 4 and 5 deal with such evidence.

105 King, *Evolving God,* Chapter 7; Dean H. Hamer, *The God Gene: How Faith is Hardwired Into Our Genes* (New York: Doubleday, 2004); Andrew Newberg, Eugene d'Aquili, and Vince Rause, *Why God Won't Go Away: Brain Science and the Biology of Belief* (New York: Ballantine, 2001).

106 King, *Evolving God*, 212.

[107] "The Confessions of St. Augustine" in NPNF1, 1, 45.

[108] Alister E. McGrath, *The Christian Theology Reader* (New York: Wiley, 2009), 577-579, "Karl Barth on Christianity and Religion"; Dietrich Bonhoeffer, *Letters and Papers from Prison*, The Enlarged Edition (New York: Macmillan, New York, 1972), 369.

[109] This is how Dorothy Sayers described a common misconception about the meaning of subscription to the creeds in *The Mind of the Maker* (London: Methuen, 1941), 12.

[110] George L. Murphy, *The Cosmos in the Light of the Cross*, Chapter 11 (Harrisburg, Pennsylvania: Trinity Press International, 2003).

[111] "The Small Catechism" in Robert Kolb and Timothy Wengert, eds., *The Book of Concord: The Confessions of the Evangelical Lutheran Church* (Minneapolis: Fortress Press, 2000), 351-354.

[112] *The Interpreter's Dictionary of the Bible* (Nashville: Abingdon Press, 1962), *s.v.* "Sin, sinners" by S. J. De Vries.

[113] Brevard S. Childs, *Myth and Reality in the Old Testament* (Naperville, Illinois: Alec R. Allenson, 1960), 67-70.

[114] Quoted in Herman Finer, "Towards a Democratic Theory" in *The American Political Science Review*, 38.2 (1945): 249.

[115] Reinhold Niebuhr, *Love and Justice: Selections from the Shorter Writings of Reinhold Niebuhr*, ed. D. B. Robertson (Philadelphia: Westminster, 1957), 48.

[116] Valerie Saiving, "The Human Situation: A Feminine View" in *The Journal of Religion* 40.2 (1960): 100. Subsequently Wanda Warren Berry, "Images of Sin and Salvation" in *Anglican Theological Review* LX (1978): 25, pointed out that Kiekegaard designated "the despair of womanliness" as "the sin of weakness" in *The Sickness Unto Death*.

[117] Especially helpful because of their engagement with a theology of the cross are Cynthia S. W. Crysdale, *Embracing Travail: Retrieving the Cross Today* (New York: Continuum, 1999), and Deanna A. Thompson, *Crossing the Divide: Luther, Feminism, and the Cross* (Minneapolis: Fortress Press, 2004).

[118] Thompson, *Crossing the Divide*, 105-108.

[119] Karl Barth, *Church Dogmatics* IV.1 (Edinburgh: T & T Clark, 1956), 142-144.

[120] For such arguments against Christianity see, e.g., H. G. Wells, *The Outline of History – Being a Plain History of Life and Mankind*, 4th ed. (London: Cassell & Co., 1926), 616. Typical uses to attack evolution can be found in Ken Ham, *The Lie: Evolution* (El Cajon, Caifornia: Master Books, 1987), 73; and Wilbert H. Rusch Sr., *Origins: What is at Stake?* (Terre Haute, Indiana: Creation Research Society Books, 1991), 25-26.

[121] Jonathan Edwards, *The Great Christian Doctrine of Original Sin Defended* in Clyde A. Holbrook, ed., Volume 3 of *The Works of Jonathan Edwards* (New Haven, Conneticuit: Yale University Press, 1970).

[122] Tatha Wiley, *Original Sin: Origins, Developments, Contemporary Meanings* (New York: Paulist, 2002), 5.

[123] Reinhold Niebuhr, *The Nature and Destiny of Man*, Vol. 1 (New York: Charles Scribner's Sons, 1964); Stephanus Trooster, *Evolution and the Doctrine of Original Sin* (New York: Newman Press, 1968); Philip Hefner, *The Human Factor: Evolution, Culture and Religion* (Minneapolis: Fortress Press, 1993); Patricia A. Williams, *Doing Without Adam and Eve: Sociobiology and Original Sin* (Minneapolis: Fortress Press, 2001); Tatha Wiley, *Original Sin*; Robin Collins, "Evolution and Original Sin," Chapter 20, in

Keith B. Miller, ed., *Perspectives on an Evolving Creation* (Grand Rapids: Grand Rapids: Wm. B. Eerdmans Publishing Co., 2003); Denis O. Lamoureux, *Evolutionary Creation: A Christian Approach to Evolution* (Eugene, Oregon: Wipf & Stock, 2008) are a few references.

[124] E.g., Williams, *Doing Without Adam and Eve.*

[125] Peter C. Bouteneff, *Beginnings: Ancient Christian Readings of the Biblical Creation Narratives* (Grand Rapids: Baker, 2008), 20, 83.

[126] Cf. James D. G. Dunn, *Word Biblical Commentary, Volume 38: Romans 1-8* (Dallas: Word, 1988), 289-290.

[127] For an exposition of this idea see John Murray, *The Imputation of Adam's Sin* (Grand Rapids: Grand Rapids: Wm. B. Eerdmans Publishing Co., 1959). One questionable aspect of it is its implication that God is the creator of the sinful condition of all humanity. As we will see in Chapter VII, imputation of the righteousness of Christ to sinners is not a legal fiction because God's word has creative effect and does what it says. If imputation of Adam's sin to his posterity paralleled this, then by declaring all Adam's descendants guilty of his sin, God in fact *made* them sinners.

[128] Wiley, *Original Sin*, Part I, sketches the history. An older work, F. R. Tennant, *The Sources of the Doctrines of the Fall and Original Sin* (New York: Schocken, 1968, reprint of the 1903 edition) provides a more detailed discussion.

[129] Relevant writings of Augustine are collected as *Saint Augustine's Anti-Pelagian Works* in NPNF 1, V. For Pelagius see B. R. Rees, *The Letters of Pelagius and his Followers* (Woodbridge, UK: Boydell, 1991).

[130] E.g., Chapter 27, Book I, of "On Marriage and Concupiscence" in *Saint Augustine's Anti-Pelagian Works*, NPNF 1, V, 274-275.

[131] Available at http://www.reformed.org/documents/canons_of_orange.html.

[132] In Roman Catholic teaching this is not true of Mary because she was preserved from "original guilt" at her conception "in consideration of the merits of Christ Jesus the Saviour of mankind." Cf. Henry Bettenson and Chris Maunder, eds., *Documents of the Christian Church,* 3rd ed. (New York: Oxford University Press, 1998), 286.

[133] This is the first part of Article IX in *The Book of Common Prayer* (New York: Church Publishing, 1979), 869. This article, now placed in the "Historical Documents" section of the prayer book of the Episcopal Church in the United States, was taken over from that approved by Parliament for the Church of England in 1571.

[134] Formula of Concord, Article I of the Epitome and of the Solid Declaration in Kolb and Wengert, eds., *The Book of Concord*, 487-491, 531-542.

[135] Heinrich Schmid, *The Doctrinal Theology of the Evangelical Lutheran Church*, 3d ed., revised (Minneapolis: Augsburg Publishing House, 1961), 220.

[136] There is such a picture of the primordial human in Ezekiel 28:11-19, but it is used as "broken myth" to describe the King of Tyre's fate.

[137] Bouteneff, *Beginnings*, provides a detailed survey.

[138] Theophilus of Antioch, "Theophilus to Autolycus" in ANF II, 104.

[139] Irenaeus of Lyons, On the Apostolic Preaching (Crestwood, New York: St. Vladimir's Seminary, 1997), 47.

[140] Timothy Ware, *The Orthodox Church* (Baltimore: Penguin, 1963), 224-230. The quotation is on page 228.

[141] Cf. Daryl P. Domning, "A New Interpretation of Original Sin" in Dr. Daryl P. Domning P. Domning and Dr. Joseph F. Wimmer, *Evolution and Original Sin: Accounting for Evil in the World* (Herndon, Virginia: Congregational Resource Guide, 2008)

[142] Reinhold Niebuhr, *The Nature and Destiny of Man*, Volume 1, Human Nature (New York: Charles Scribner's Sons, 1964), 150.

[143] Pierre Teilhard de Chardin, "Note on Some Possible Historical Representations of Original Sin" in *Christianity and Evolution* (New York: Harcourt Brace Jovanovich, 1969), 51-52.

[144] G. B. Caird, *The Revelation of St. John the Divine* (New York: Harper & Row, 1966), 168, argues for the translation, "the Lamb slaughtered from the foundation of the world" (cf. KJV and NRSV margin) in Revelation 13:8.

[145] "The Augsburg Confession—German Text—Article II" in Kolb and Wengert, eds., *The Book of Concord*, 38.

[146] Ted Peters, *Playing God? Genetic Determinism and Human Freedom* (New York: Routledge, 1997).

[147] Cf. Trooster, *Evolution and the Doctrine of Original Sin.*

[148] *The Interpreter's Dictionary of the Bible, s.v.* "Sin, sinners" by S. J. De Vries, 371.

[149] Paul Tillich, "You Are Accepted" in *The Shaking of the Foundations* (New York: Charles Scribner's Sons, 1948), 155.

[150] See, e.g., the descriptions of reactions of gorillas and chimpanzees to the deaths of members of their groups in Barbara J. King, *Evolving God: A Provocative View on the Origins of Religion* (New York: Doubleday, 2007), 59-60.

[151] C. S. Lewis, *Out of the Silent Planet* (New York: Macmillan, 1965), 158-159.

[152] George L. Murphy, *The Trademark of God* (Wilton, Conneticuit: Morehouse-Barlow, 1986), 61-62.

[153] George L. Murphy, "Prolepsis and the Physics of Retrocausality" in *Theology and Science* 7 (2009): 213.

[154] Gerhard von Rad, *Old Testament Theology* (New York: Harper & Row, 1962), 1:136-139, 175-179.

[155] Hymns 199 and 200 in *The Hymnal 1982* (New York: Church Publishing, 1985).

[156] Brevard S. Childs, *Myth and Reality in the Old Testament* (Naperville, Illinois: Alec R. Allenson, 1960), especially page 42.

[157] Hermann Gunkel, *Schöpfung und Chaos in Urzeit und Endzeit* (Göttingen: Vandenhoeck und Ruprecht, 1895); John Day, *God's Conflict with the Dragon and the Sea* (New York: Cambridge, 1985); Bernhard W. Anderson, *Creation Versus Chaos* (Philadelphia: Fortress Press, 1987); George L. Murphy, "The Sea of Chaos and Creation," presented at the 2000 meeting of the American Scientific Affiliation.

[158] G. B. Caird, *The Revelation of St. John the Divine* (New York: Harper & Row, 1966), 279-280.

[159] Rudolf Bultmann, *The Second Letter to the Corinthians* (Minneapolis: Augsburg Publishing House, 1985), 145, 156-158.

[160] Eduard Lohse, *Colossians and Ephesians* (Philadelphia: Fortress Press, 1971) is right in arguing (pages 60-61) that the viewpoint of the theology of the cross should be retained

in the Colossians text, but the claim that only the salvation of humanity is in view is unjustified. Nor is there good reason to limit the significance of Romans 8:18-25 by labeling verses19-22 as "an apocalyptic fragment," as in John Reumann, *Creation and New Creation: The Past, Present, and Future of God's Creative Activity* (Minneapolis: Augsburg Publishing House, 1973), 89-99.

[161] E. Schillebeeckx, "I Believe in Jesus of Nazareth" in *Listening* 15 (1980): 159.

[162] Paul Tillich, *The New Being* (New York: Charles Scribner's Sons, 1955), 15-24.

[163] Dietrich Bonhoeffer, "Creation and Fall" in *Dietrich Bonhoeffer Works*, Volume 3 (Minneapolis: Fortress Press, 1997), 34-35.

[164] One exception is Peter Schmiechen, *Saving Power: Theories of Atonement and Forms of the Church* (Grand Rapids: Wm. B. Eerdmans Publishing Co., 2005), 194-221, where Anselm's view is discussed under the heading "The Restoration of the Creation."

[165] Anselm of Canterbury, "Why God Became Man" in Eugene R. Fairweather, ed., *A Scholastic Miscellany: Anselm to Ockham* (New York: Macmillan, 1970), 125-126.

[166] St. Athanasius, "On the Incarnation of the Word" in NPNF 2, IV, 38.

[167] *Ibid.*, 43.

[168] *Ibid.*, 40.

[169] Irenaeus, "Against Heresies" II, xxii, 4 in ANF I, 391.

[170] Gustaf Wingren, *Man and the Incarnation* (London: Oliver and Boyd, 1959), 173-174.

[171] Gerd Theissen, *Biblical Faith: An Evolutionary Approach* (Philadelphia: Fortress Press, 1985), is a helpful attempt to understand this development in evolutionary terms.

[172] G. H. Box, *The Apocalypse of Abraham,* Appendix I (London: Society for Propagation of Christian Knowledge, 1919), 92; Sura VI of the Qur'an, vv.74-79 in *The Holy Qur'an*, 3rd ed., with Arabic text and English translation and commentary by Abdullah Yusuf Ali (Damascus: Dar Al-Mushaf, 1938), 309-310; George L. Murphy, *The Cosmos in the Light of the Cross* (Harrisburg, Pennsylvania: Trinity Press International, 2003), 20-21.

[173] Stephen Jay Gould, *Wonderful Life: The Burgess Shale and the Nature of History* (New York: W.W. Norton, 1989).

[174] Robert H. Gundry, "The Use of the Old Testament in St. Matthew's Gospel," NovTSup 18 (Leiden: Brill, 1967), 139-140, presents the case for reading the Greek as "seventy-seven" rather than "seventy times seven."

[175] *The Hymnal 1982*, hymn 544.

[176] Cf. Horace D. Hummel, *The Word Becoming Flesh: An Introduction to the Origin, Purpose, and Meaning of the Old Testament* (St. Louis: Concordia Publishing House, 1979).

[177] E.g., John R. Hinnels, "Zoroastrian Influence on Biblical Imagery" in *Zoroastriam and Parsi Studies: Selected Works of John R. Hinnels* (Burlington, Vermont: Ashgate, 2000), 27-92.

[178] Karl Barth, *Der Römerbrief*, 4th ed. (Munich: Chr. Kaiser, 1924), 6.

[179] Henry Bettenson and Chris Maunder (ed.), *Documents of the Christian Church*, 3rd ed. (New York: Oxford, 1999), 56.

[180] Thomas G. Weinandy, O.F.M. Cap., *In the Likeness of Sinful Flesh: An Essay on the Humanity of Christ* (Edinburgh: T& T Clark, 1993). For the difference here between

Greek and Latin theologies see Thomas F. Torrance, *The Christian Frame of Mind* (Colorado Springs: Helmers & Howard, 1989), 6-11.

[181] Karl Barth, *Church Dogmatics* IV.2 (Edinburgh: T & T Clark, 1958), 92.

[182] The role of the Spirit is emphasized in Weinandy, *In the Likeness of Sinful Flesh.* See especially 59-61, 94-102, and 150-151.

[183] From Burton Raffel's translation of the third of the Anglo-Saxon "Advent Lyrics" in *Poems from the Old English*, 2nd ed. (Lincoln, Nebraska: University of Nebraska, 1964), 67.

[184] John Calvin, *Institutes of the Christian Religion* 2.16.5 (Philadelphia: Westminster, 1960). Volume I, 507. Cf. Also William C. Placher, "How Does Jesus Save?" in *Christian Century* 126.11 (2009): 23.

[185] Luke Timothy Johnson, *The Creed: What Christians Believe and Why it Matters* (New York: Doubleday, 2003), 161

.[186] There was, however, thought to be an inferior mode of divine communication, the *bath qol*, or "daughter of a voice." Cf. R. Travers Herford, "Pirke Aboth" in R.H. Charles, ed., *The Apocrypha and Pseudepigrapha of the Old Testament,* Vol. II (Berkeley: Apocryphile, 2004, a reprint of the 1913 Oxford edition), 711.

[187] Raymond E. Brown, *The Gospel According to John I-XII* (New York: Doubleday, 1966), 172.

[188] Pinchas Lapide, *The Resurrection of Jesus: A Jewish Perspective* (Minneapolis: Augsburg, 1983).

[189] Irenaeus, "Against Heresies" II, xxii, 4 in ANF I, 391.

[190] Gerhard O. Forde, "The Work of Christ," Seventh Locus in Carl E. Braaten and Robert W. Jenson, eds., *Christian Dogmatics*, Vol.2 (Philadelphia: Fortress Press, 1984).

[191] *Ibid.*, 79-99.

[192] *Ibid.*, 9.

[193] "The Large Catechism"in Robert Kolb and Timothy Wengert, eds., *The Book of Concord: The Confessions of the Evangelical Lutheran Church* (Minneapolis: Fortress Press, 2000), 386.

[194] Heinrich Schmid, *The Doctrinal Theology of the Evangelical Lutheran Church*, 3rd ed., revised (Minneapolis: Augsburg Publishing House, 1961), 410-418.

[195] For Luther's distinction between the "proper work" which corresponds to God's true character and the "alien work" which is foreign to it but is done to make the proper work possible, see, e.g., Paul Althaus, *The Theology of Martin Luther* (Philadelphia: Fortress, 1966), 120, 171-172.

[196] Ludwig Hofacker, quoted by William Malcolm Macgregor in John W. Doberstein, ed., *Minister's Prayer Book* (Philadelphia: Fortress Press, n.d.), 403.

[197] Kent S. Knutson, *His Only Son Our Lord* (Minneapolis: Augsburg Publishing House, 1966), 72-75.

[198] George L. Murphy, "Atonement as Fiducial Influence" in *Currents in Theology and Mission* 37.1 (2010): 23.

[199] Forde, "The Work of Christ," 79.

[200] Anselm of Canterbury, "Why God Became Man" in Eugene R. Fairweather, ed., *A Scholastic Miscellany: Anselm to Ockham* (New York: Macmillan, 1970), 182.

[201] Gerhard O. Forde, *On Being a Theologian of the Cross: Reflections on Luther's Heidelberg Disputation, 1518* (Grand Rapids: Wm. B. Eerdmans Publishing Co., 1997), 112.

[202] Johann Wolfgang von Goethe, *Faust: A Tragedie*, trans. Alice Raphael (New York: Heritage Press, 1932), 46.

[203] For the history see J. N. D. Kelly, *Early Christian Creeds*, 3rd ed. (New York: Continuum, 1972), 378 – 383. Kelly comments (page 378, note 3) that instead of *inferna*, "[t]he form *inferos* is nowadays preferred as indicating that the place of the departed, not the damned, is meant." A brief presentation of the rationale of the International Consultation on English Texts for its rendering of the phrase is its *Prayers We Have in Common*, 2nd revised ed. (Philadelphia: Fortress Press, 1975), 4-5.

[204] An important early reference is "The Gospel of Nicodemus, Part II. The Descent of Christ into Hell" in ANF VIII, 435-458. The medieval description of the harrowing of hell in William Langland, *Piers the Ploughman*, Book XVIII (New York: Penguin, 1966), also presents an idea of atonement as Christ's payment of his soul to the devil to redeem sinners.

[205] E.g., Doris Wild, *Holy Icons* (Berne: Hallwag, 1961), Plate XVI.

[206] Elliot, in R. A. Martin, *James*, and John H. Elliott, *I-II Peter, Jude* (Minneapolis: Augsburg Publishing House, 1982) points out (page 98) that, in view of similarities between this passage and 1 Enoch, it is possible that what is envisioned is Christ's preaching during his *ascent* through the heavens where the "disobedient spirits" are imprisoned.

[207] Two older studies of Luther's views on the descent are Erich Vogelsang, *Der Angefochtene Christus Bei Luther* (Berlin: Walter de Gruyter, 1932), 44-52, and Paul Althaus, "Niedergefahren zur Hölle" in *Zeitschrift für systematische Theologie* 19 (1942): 365.

[208] Heinrich Heppe, *Reformed Dogmatics: Set Out and Illustrated from the Sources* (Grand Rapids: Baker, 1978), 490-494; David Lauber, *Barth on the Descent into Hell: God, Atonement and the Christian Life* (Aldershot UK: Ashgate, 2004), 1-41.

[209] Hans Urs von Balthasar, *Mysterium Paschale* (Grand Rapids: Wm. B. Eerdmans Publishing Co., 1993), especially Chapter 4; Alyssa Lyra Pitstick, *Light in Darkness: Hans Urs von Balthasar and the Catholic Doctrine of Christ's Descent into Hell* (Grand Rapids: Wm. B. Eerdmans Publishing Co., 2007); Lauber, *Barth on the Descent into Hell*, also treats Balthasar's approach.

[210] Article IX of the Thorough Declaration of the Formula of Concord in *Concordia Triglotta*, (St. Louis: Concordia Publishing House, 1921), 1048-1052. The German text of this older edition of the *Book of Concord* includes the relevant portion of Luther's sermon.

[211] Dietrich Bonhoeffer, "Creation and Fall" in *Dietrich Bonhoeffer Works*, Volume 3 (Minneapolis: Fortress Press, 1997), 35.

[212] "Savior of the Nations, Come," hymn 28 in *Lutheran Book of Worship* (Minneapolis: Augsburg, 1978), verses 4 and 5.

[213] I am indebted to Professor Duane Priebe for this description.

[214] "The Augsburg Confession, German Text, Article IV: Justification" in Robert Kolb and Timothy Wengert, eds., *The Book of Concord: The Confessions of the Evangelical Lutheran Church* (Minneapolis: Fortress Press, 2000), 38 & 40.

215 "Confutatio Pontificia" in M. Reu, *The Augsburg Confession: A Collection of Sources with An Historical Introduction,* Second Part (St. Louis: Concordia, 1983 reprint of the 1930 Wartburg edition), 350-351.

216 The declaration may be found at http://www.elca.org/Who-We-Are/Our-Three-Expressions/Churchwide-Organization Office-of-the-Presiding-Bishop/Ecumenical-and-Inter-Religious-Relations/Bilateral-Conversations/Lutheran-Roman-Catholic/The-Joint-Declaration.aspx.

217 Carl E. Braaten and Robert W. Jenson, eds., *Union with Christ: The New Finnish Interpretation of Luther* (Grand Rapids: Wm. B. Eerdmans Publishing Co., 1998). Stephen Westerholm, *Perspectives Old and New on Paul: The "Lutheran" Paul and His Critics* (Grand Rapids: Wm. B. Eerdmans Publishing Co., 2004).

218 An earlier version of the following discussion is George L. Murphy, "Restating Justification for a Scientific World," *Trinity Seminary Review* 30 (2009): 103.

219 Paul Tillich, *The Protestant Era,* abridged edition (Chicago: University of Chicago Press, 1957), 196.

220 Quoted by Carl E. Braaten, who describes this outcome as a "fiasco" and "farce," in *Principles of Lutheran Theology* (Philadelphia: Fortress Press, 1983), 38-39.

221 Richard Dawkins, *The God Delusion* (Boston: Houghton-Mifflin, 2006); Victor J. Stenger, *God The Failed Hypothesis. How Science Shows That God Does Not Exist* (Amherst, New York: Prometheus, 2007).

222 Karl Barth, *Church Dogmatics* IV.1 (Edinburgh: T.& T. Clark, 1956), § 59.2.

223 Stephen F. Mason, *A History of the Sciences,* New Revised Edition (New York: Collier, 1962), 171-172.

224 George L. Murphy, "What Can We Learn from Einstein about Religious Language?" in *Currents in Theology and Mission* 15 (1988): 342.

225 "The Apology of the Augsburg Confession" in Robert Kolb and Timothy Wengert, eds., *The Book of Concord,* 132.

226 *Ibid.,* 133. A very similar statement is on page 139.

227 "The Solid Declaration" of "The Formula of Concord," Article III in Kolb and Wengert, *The Book of Concord,* 565.

228 *Ibid.*

229 *Ibid.,* 565-566.

230 Heinrich Schmid, *The Doctrinal Theology of the Evangelical Lutheran Church,* 3rd ed., revised (Minneapolis: Augsburg Publishing House, 1961), 441-461.

231 "The Solid Declaration of The Formula of Concord," Article III in Kolb and Wengert, *The Book of Concord,* 565.

232 George L. Murphy, *The Cosmos in the Light of the Cross* (Harrisburg, Pennsylvania: Trinity Press International, 2003), Chapter 6.

233 George L. Murphy, *The Trademark of God* (Wilton, Conneticuit: Morehouse-Barlow, 1986).

234 Murphy, *The Cosmos in the Light of the Cross,* 106-108.

235 Cf. Rudolf Bultmann, *Theology of the New Testament,* Vol. 1 (New York: Charles Scribner's Sons, 1951), 274-279.

[236] A. Tanquerey and J. B. Bord, *Manual of Dogmatic Theology,* Vol. 2 (New York: Desclee, 1959), 120-130.

[237] E.g., Irenaeus, "Against Heresies" IV.20.1 in ANF I, 487. Note also the epiclesis of Eucharistic Prayer I, Holy Eucharist I, *The Book of Common Prayer* (New York: Church Publishing, 1979), 335: "vouchsafe to bless and sanctify, with thy Word and Holy Spirit, these thy gifts and creatures of bread and wine. . . ."

[238] "The Litany" in *Lutheran Book of Worship* (Minneapolis: Augsburg Publishing House, 1978), 171.

[239] "The Small Catechism" in Kolb and Wengert, *The Book of Concord,* 355.

[240] Murphy, *The Cosmos in the Light of the Cross,* 75.

[241] G. C. Berkouwer, quoted in Benjamin Wirt Farley, *The Providence of God* (Grand Rapids: Baker, 1988), 37.

[242] Murphy, *The Cosmos in the Light of the Cross,* 77.

[243] "The Small Catechism" in Kolb and Wengert, *The Book of Concord,* 360.

[244] John T. McNeill, ed., *Calvin: Institutes of the Christian Religion,* Vol. 2 (Westminster: Philadelphia, 1960), 966; "The Solid Declaration of The Formula of Concord," Article II, in Kolb and Wengert, *The Book of Concord,* 543-562.

[245] Cf. St. Augustine, "Tractate LXXX on the Gospel of St. John" in NPNF 1, VII, 344: "Take away the word, and the water is neither more nor less than water. The word is added to the element, and there results the Sacrament, as if itself also a kind of visible word." Robert W. Jenson discusses the sacraments under this rubric in *Visible Words* (Philadelphia: Fortress Press, 1978).

[246] Thomas Aquinas, *Summa Theologica,* First Part, Q. 106, Art.1 (Chicago: Encyclopedia Britannica, 1952), 544, affirms that "the justification of the unrighteous" is done by God alone but argues that it is not, properly speaking, a miracle because it could not be brought about by another cause. Obviously one's definition of "miracle" is critical here.

[247] A.R. Peacocke, *Science and the Christian Experiment* (New York: Oxford, 1971), Chapter 7.

[248] Pierre Teilhard de Chardin, *Christianity and Evolution* (New York: Harcourt Brace Jovanovich, 1969), 16, 66-72; George L. Murphy, "The Church in Evolution" in *Seminary Ridge Review* 5 (2002): 380.

[249] Pierre Teilhard de Chardin, *Activation of Energy* (New York: Harcourt Brace Jovanovich, 1970), 115-116. See also the story sermon "I am Christ's Body" in George L. Murphy, *Pulpit Science Fiction* (Lima, Ohio: CSS, 2005).

[250] James A. Nestingen and Gerhard O. Forde, *Free to Be: A Handbook to Luther's Small Catechism* (Minneapolis: Augsburg Publishing House, 1975), 113-115.

[251] "The Small Catechism" in Kolb and Wengert, *The Book of Concord,* 355-356.

[252] William Butler Yeats, "Calvary" in *Selected Poems and Plays of William Butler Yeats* (New York: Collier, 1966). The sentence is repeated three times on pages 194-195.

[253] H. Paul Santmire, *The Travail of Nature: The Ambiguous Ecological Promise of Christian Theology* (Philadelphia: Fortress Press, 1985). The same author's later books, *Nature Reborn: The Ecological and Cosmic Promise of Christian Theology* (Minneapolis: Fortress Press, 2000) and *Ritualizing Nature: Renewing Christian Liturgy in a Time of Crisis* (Minneapolis: Fortress Press, 2008) offer a positive vision.

254 Karl Rahner, "Natural Science and Reasonable Faith: Theological Perspectives for Dialogue with the Natural Sciences" in *Theological Investigations XXI* (New York: Crossroad, 1988), 54.

255 Rudolf Bultmann, *Jesus Christ and Mythology* (New York: Charles Scribner's Sons, 1958), 69.

256 http://www.goodreads.com/author/quotes/10538.Carl_Sagan.

257 I heard the claim about Eve and thermodynamics in a talk but withhold the occasion to avoid embarrassing anyone. The Second Law is involved in (among other things) chemical reactions that are crucial for life. Entropy is not in itself bad; see, e.g., Robert John Russell, "Entropy & Evil," *Zygon* 19 (1984): 449.

258 St. Cyprian, "Cyprian to Jubaium" in *The Fathers of the Church,* Volume 51 (Washington: The Catholic University of America, 1964), 282.

259 Karl Rahner, "Anonymous Christians," "Christianity and Non-Christian Religions," and "Atheism and Implicit Christianity" in Gerald A. McCool, ed., *A Rahner Reader* (New York: Seabury, 1975), 211-224.

260 Gerhard O. Forde, "The Work of Christ" in Carl E. Braaten and Robert W. Jenson, ed., *Christian Dogmatics* (Philadelphia: Fortress Press, 1984), 93.

261 Pierre Teilhard de Chardin, *The Divine Milieu* (New York: Harper & Row, 1960), 147.

262 http://www.lincolnarchives.com/LincolnQuotes.php

263 Daniel J. Sahas, *John of Damascus on Islam: "The Heresy of the Ishmaelites"* (Leiden: E. J. Brill, 1972).

264 C. S. Lewis, *The Abolition of Man* (New York: Macmillan, 1947), Appendix.

265 Robert Browning, "Holy-Cross Day" in *Poems of Robert Browning* (London: Oxford, 1949), 268-272.

266 John B. Cobb, Jr., "A Christian Critique of Pure Land Buddhism" in Dennis Hirota, ed., *Toward a Contemporary Understanding of Pure Land Buddhism: Creating a Shin Buddhist Theology in a Religiously Plural World* (Albany, New York: State University of New York, 2000), 147-160. Other essays in the volume give more detail on Pure Land Buddhism.

267 Quoted in Edith Hamilton, *Mythology* (New York: Mentor, 1953), 309.

268 St. Justin Martyr, "The First Apology of Justin" in ANF I, 178.

269 L. W. Barnard, *Justin Martyr: His Life and Thought* (London: Cambridge University Press, 1967), 85.

270 Plato, "Phaedo" 64a, in Benjamin Jowett, *The Dialogues of Plato*, 3rd ed., Vol. 2 (New York: Macmillan, 1892), 202.

271 St. Gregory Nazianzen, "To Cledonius the Priest Against Appolinarius" in NPNF 2, VII, 440.

272 George L. Murphy, *The Cosmos in the Light of the Cross* (Harrisburg, Pennsylvania: Trinity Press International, 2003), Chapter 11.

273 *Lutheran Book of Worship* (Minneapolis: Augsburg Publishing House, 1978), 68.

274 Laurie Zoloth, "Science and Ethics in Judaism" in Ted Peters and Gaymon Bennett, eds., *Bridging Science and Religion* (London: SCM Press, 2002), 219.

275 Michael J. Crowe, *The Extraterrestrial Life Debate, 1750-1900* (Mineola, New York: Dover, 1999), from which the Emerson quotation is taken, and Steven J. Dick, *Life on*

Other Worlds: The 20th-Century Extraterrestrial Life Debate (New York: Cambridge, 1998) cover the history of the discussion.

[276] Sir David Brewster, *More Worlds Than One: The Creed of the Philosopher and the Hope of the Christian* (London: John Murray, 1854).

[277] E.g., Jay M. Pasachoff and Marc L. Kutner, *University Astronomy* (Philadelphia: W. B. Saunders, 1978), 547.

[278] Alan Boss, *The Crowded Universe: The Search for Living Planets* (New York: Basic, 2009).

[279] http://www.dailymail.co.uk/sciencetech/article-1245970/The-digital-revolution-making-Earth-harder-detect-inquisitive-aliens-worlds-leading-ET-hunter-says.html.

[280] On "Fermi's paradox" see, e.g., http://www.fas.org/sgp/othergov/doe/lanl/la-10311-ms.pdf.

[281] Crowe, *The Extraterrestrial Life Debate, 1750-1900*, 116.

[282] This possibility was suggested by C. S. Lewis, "Religion and Rocketry" in *Fern-seed and Elephants: And Other Essays on Christianity* (Glasgow: Fontana/Collins, 1975), 86-95, originally published in *Christian Herald* in 1958. Lewis did not, however, rest his entire argument upon it.

[283] The remainder of this section follows George L. Murphy, "Is Anybody Out There?" in *Lutheran Partners* 23.1 (2007): 26. See also Ted Peters, "The implications of the discovery of extra-terrestrial life for religion" in *Philosophical Transactions of the Royal Society* A369 (2011): 644.

[284] C.S. Lewis, *Miracles: A Preliminary Study* (New York: Macmillan, 1947), 129.

[285] Martin Luther, "Confession Concerning Christ's Supper" in *Luther's Works*, Volume 37 (Philadelphia: Muhlenberg, 1961). Recent applications of this concept are Murphy, *The Cosmos in the Light of the Cross*, 192, and H. Paul Santmire, "So That He Might Fill All Things: Comprehending the Cosmic Love of Christ" in *dialog* 42 (2003): 257.

[286] Dick, *Life on Other Worlds*, 247-248. For a fictional treatment see George L. Murphy, "The Signal" in *Pulpit Science Fiction* (Lima, Ohio: CSS, 2005).

[287] Bultmann, *Theology of the New Testament*, Vol. 1 (New York: Charles Scribner's Sons, 1951), 274-279.

[288] George L. Murphy, "Hints from Science for Eschatology—and Vice Versa" in Carl E. Braaten and Robert W. Jenson, eds., *The Last Things: Biblical and Theological Perspectives on Eschatology* (Grand Rapids: Wm. B. Eerdmans Publishing Co., 2002), 146-168.

[289] John Polkinghorne, *The Faith of a Physicist* (Princeton: Princeton University Press, 1994, 167.

[290] Ted Peters, *Anticipating Omega* (Göttingen: Vandenhoeck & Ruprecht, 2007). The quoted sentence is on page 12

[291] George L. Murphy, "Prolepsis and the Physics of Retrocausality," *Theology and Science* 7 (2009): 213.

[292] Robert John Russell, *Cosmology, Evolution and Resurrection Hope* (Kitchener, Ontario: Pandora, 2006), 47.

[293] Gordon W. Lathrop, *Holy Ground: A Liturgical Cosmology* (Minneapolis: Fortress Press, 2003), 220-224.